Life can only be understood backward; but it must be lived forward.

—Soren Kierkegaard
Danish philosopher (1813-1855)

LIVING YOUR LIFE
BACKWARD

FINDING BALANCE BETWEEN FAMILY, MONEY & WORK

LIVING YOUR LIFE
BACKWARD

FINDING BALANCE BETWEEN FAMILY, MONEY & WORK

Reginald Daniel

with Phyllis S. Robinson

Living Your Life Backward™
Finding Balance Between Family, Money & Work
Copyright © 2007 Reginald Daniel
Published by King & Queen Publishing, LLC

For further information, please contact:

King & Queen Publishing, LLC
P.O. Box 4408
Largo, MD 20775
www.kingandqueenpublishing.com
www.livingyourlifebackward.com

Book design by:

Arbor Books, Inc.
19 Spear Road, Suite 301
Ramsey, NJ 07446
www.arborbooks.com

Printed in the United States

Living Your Life Backward™
Finding Balance Between Family, Money & Work
Reginald Daniel

1. Title 2. Author 3. Motivational/Self-Help

Library of Congress Control Number: 2006905737
ISBN: 0-9787142-0-2

Mom, you told me that I could do anything that I wanted to. I guess you can tell that I believed you. Thank you for all of the love that you give me. This is for you. I love you.

Table of Contents

Dedication

Two people have had the greatest impact on me in my life; my late stepfather, Andrew Jones, Jr., and my loving daughter. This book is dedicated to both the memory and life of Andrew and the life and existence of my daughter, who is one of the most wonderful people I have ever met.

As a young man growing up in an environment that provided little hope, Andrew Jones, Jr. began to date my mother, Nellie Daniel. The slight complication was that Nellie was divorced and had six children. Six children! That was some kind of love. Of those six, my two older sisters were adults at the time and not living with us.

That is where the journey began. From the first day I met Andrew, he treated me with kindness and love. He tried to give my brothers and me everything we needed to be men—he let us see him doing the things men do, such as paying bills and of course, being a man of few words. When those words came out, however, they were meaningful. Andrew took time with my brothers and me—that in itself was a wonderful gift.

Andrew filled the role of the father I never really knew. We were wonderful friends and both knew without a doubt that there was tremendous love between us. He was everything a boy could need to become a man. Andrew, thank you and I love you for everything you were to me.

Oh, my Little Princess. My 10-year-old daughter is the balance to the strong and silent man I learned to be. My daughter loves her daddy and has given me a perspective on family. I now understand that when you have love in abundance in your home, you have everything. You are rich beyond measure. Through her existence, my daughter has given me the gift of tenderness. In any instance where I did not respond with tenderness, either her words or actions helped redirect me to be loving and attentive in everything I did. These skills have helped me to be a more loving person in every aspect of my life.

God gave me a daughter with a loving and giving spirit, and this little person has helped shape me into the person I am today. Through the skills that I have learned from her, I am able to enjoy everyday life in ways I could not have imagined. Sweetheart, continue to be the loving person you are, and know that Daddy loves you always.

My stepfather and my daughter helped create a combination of toughness and tenderness that helped me envision and execute a work such as this book.

Special Thanks

I would like to first thank God for giving me health, strength and the vision for my life. God is great and I continue to strive to be a vessel for his love so watch out! I can't wait to see what is next.

Like any work, this is the culmination of many kinds of supportive acts. I am sure that I cannot name all of the people that helped me get to this point in my life, so I will focus on those that were involved with this project. First I would like to thank Phyllis S. Robinson. Phyllis, I think we make a great team. Thanks for putting your heart into this book. I am glad that we could share this experience. Dr. Susan Newman, thank you for your guidance, hard work and support. I really appreciate everything that you did on this project and for your friendship. Don Cryer. Your friendship, prayers and encouragement are priceless, thank you. Dr. Latanya Brown, your review of the economics section was extremely valuable, thank you. Latonya Blige Dacosta, your knowledge is vast and I really appreciate all of the tips that you gave me and your continued friendship, thank you very much. Thank you, Valorie Burton for your valuable insights. Thanks Diana Riley for your help. I would like to thank my readers: Pastor Jack Morris, Marissa Daniel, Chon and Wyatt Chase, Dr. Tepy Kong, Gary Thompson,

Karen Lewis, Donald Cryer, Gary Murray, and Dr. Ronald Williams. Thank you, Chioma, for all of the love and support that you gave me through the process and for volunteering to write the abstract. Great Job!

My siblings Gwen, Brenda, Kevin, Gregory, and Steven, I love you all. Mom, you are the greatest!

God Bless you.

Introduction

This book will take you on a journey. It will help you to find one of the most elusive treasures available to mankind, balance. The place where we feel all of our steps are aligned and every day has purpose. In this place of balance, we find that we actually have some degree of control of our time.

I am sure you have heard or even used the phrase, "Life is short." Well, it is. I am also sure this is not a revelation. On our journey we will address this reality head on. Depending upon your age and experience, you have seen things that have placed this reality either in the forefront of your mind, or made it a distant concern. If we allow ourselves to pay attention, life events tend to introduce us to our mortality. We do, in fact, get to choose when we accept this reality. One thing is for certain—we do not get a free pass. We must deal with this issue at some point.

I was once told by a wise man that there are two life-changing experiences: the death of a loved one and the birth of a child. He said that the death of a loved one is more life changing. For me, it was the death of my natural father. This introduced me to the concept of mortality in a way I could not have imagined. During the beginning of the mourning process, I felt that my heart was being dragged slowly through my body with a hook, from my chest to my feet. With each movement of my heart through my body, I felt excruciating emotional pain, the likes of which I could never have prepared for.

Unfortunately, accompanying the hurt of losing my father was the feeling of regret. After he and my mother divorced, when I was about three years old, I spent years telling myself that I would get to know him when I could show him what he had missed out on. That time would be after I received my honorable discharge from the Air Force and landed a very good job. He did not cooperate with my plan and died a premature death at the age of 50.

This book is not about death; it is in fact about life. What better way to appreciate your life than to think about the day it could end? I do not want you to experience any of the kind of regret I dealt with when my father died.

From this day forward you will "Live Your Life Backward." You will make every decision with the outcome in mind. You will write your eulogy through this process—today. You will know beyond the shadow of a doubt that your loved ones will have loving memories of the times you shared. You will embrace the people most important to you with the greatest form of passion. You will make them a top priority in your plans and ultimately, your daily decisions and actions.

One important component to a successful life is the mastery of the economic part of living. This is not an attempt to tell you how to get rich, nor is it an attempt to convince you to be an entrepreneur or anything like that. I only want to help you have the best life you can, and a big part of living is money. If we do not accept this fact, we are simply burying our heads in the sand. We make decisions on such things as what kind of houses we want to live in, what kinds of cars we want to drive, or even what kinds of watches or clothes we want to wear. These decisions impact the most important aspect of our lives—our relationships with the ones we love and cherish the most.

With proper focus and planning, we can put first things first. We can spend time with our aging parents. We can make the children's soccer games and we can make each and every piano recital. I am not just telling you this because I think these are interesting theories; I am telling you this because I did it. I did these things while building a successful technology company.

The death of my father left me with a feeling of regret so deep that I knew I never wanted to feel it again. From the time I was 25, I made every decision with my family in mind, including the child who was not even born at the time. My objective was simple— to make enough money to support my wife, to be discovered, and give her the ability to be a stay at home mom if she so desired. Once I understood these objectives, I began to live my life backward. I put a price on this dream. I quit jobs where I made a lot of money, felt really secure, and probably could have worked there for 10 to 15 years. I quit these jobs because they did not work with my life plan. They would not allow me to achieve the objectives I had put in place for the family I hoped for.

Even though things did not go exactly as I planned with my marriage, at least I was in a position to manage my schedule as a divorced, single dad in a manner that allowed me still to be a good parent. Achieving these objectives in my life required honest self-assessment, goal setting, planning, and taking my objectives seriously. I cannot understate the importance of successfully dealing with the economic elements of living.

I invite you to begin the process of living your life backward. If nothing else, it will be a good opportunity for you to decide what is most important in your life. I guarantee you will be blessed through the experience. I must admit I have been blessed in ways that I could have never imagined.

God bless you and let's enjoy the journey.

CHAPTER ONE
THE PATH OF MONEY

He who will not economize will have to agonize.

—Confucius

If you were to go on a 300-mile drive across the country to visit family or friends, would you first take out a map to study your journey? Would you figure out where you were currently on the map, locate your destination, and then chart a course? If you did not write the route down on paper or highlight the map, you would at least understand in your mind what path you planned to take. Additionally, you would possibly mention to your spouse or children your path of choice and at a minimum, how long the journey would take.

You have just purchased a dollhouse for your five-year-old daughter. You open the box and it has what seems to be 10,000 pieces. In reality, there are only 40 pieces, but your sweet daughter is gazing at Daddy with love and anticipation, convinced it will take you only 30 seconds to put it all together. You, on the other hand, are trying to figure out how all the pieces should fit together. Faltering, you begin picking up one piece at a time. Forty-five minutes later, after your daughter has fallen asleep on the floor—complete adoration for you still intact—you *finally* pick up the instructions. Therein lie the answers to all of your questions, and you discover exactly what each piece is for. After a solid 15 minutes of directed efforts, you wake your angel and she gives her hero a great big hug, saying, "Thank you, Daddy."

What do these little anecdotes have to do with money? How will these stories help improve your economic position in life? Well, money is one of the most disrespected elements of our lives today. Money can be a tremendous asset and help our families enjoy a wonderful quality of life. Or, it can be a horrible liability and force us to endure the pain of meeting obligations that apply a tremendous level of stress to everyday living. This can be very painful to you and those family members who have to spend time around you. How do we get money to have a positive impact on our lives? How do we manage not to get stressed out by having to deal with it?

Always Have a Plan

As in the cross-country journey, where you take out the map and share the elements of the trip with your family, I advocate taking the same approach with money. Set economic objectives for your family. Everyone possible should be onboard with the financial objectives. And of course, understand how money works.

Another area to spend time on, is the understanding of contracts. Reading them is very important, and not understanding them can be very painful. Before you engage in financial agreements, understand the total terms. Understand how they can impact your family positively or negatively. You do not want your five-year-old daughter to look up at you, totally confused about what she has done wrong because you have just snapped at her. Why did you snap? Because she has just asked when she could go shopping for new school clothes. I do not want you to feel the financial frustration that can lead to this stress.

I am not suggesting that in order to have success with money, you have to have a master's in business administration or an economics degree. I am, however, suggesting that this become an area of life you take seriously. You should have a basic understanding of money as a tool, and how it can work for you and your family to help you have a good quality of life.

Understanding Your Personal Economics

It is not my intent to give you a financial handbook. There are professionals who can provide quality financial services to you and your family. Instead, I want to help you develop a life strategy, and within that strategy will be one that deals with finances.

What does the word "economics" mean to you? Do your eyes glaze over when you hear it? Do you react with that "Huh?" look because it's too confusing? Maybe you're a hairsplitting step ahead of the mainstream—barely sliding through the only economics course you've ever taken.

For the majority of Americans, the word "economics" means nothing at all. It's too complicated—it's vague gibberish that politicians throw around during elections. Face it: Most of us are not familiar with the concept of economics, and we're comfortable with the term "money." Economics is complex. Money is concrete. So we hear the term "economics," then we trash it, with no thought in between. "Thank you very much for that speech, Mr. Political wannabe," we say, "but I live in the REAL world. There are bills to pay and I've got to get to work."

So you get to work. And there's your boss, throwing that "economics" word around again, announcing, "Due to a downward spiral in the American economy, your pay is being cut 25 percent." Instinctively, you begin calculating the impact this decrease will have on you, your family, and your life. Do you have to forget the Bahamas cruise, start carpooling to work, or nix Jennifer's ballet class? Welcome to real-world economics. Without meaning to, you've just connected money and economics.

Not All Choices Will Be Easy

Let's not bypass the real issue here—the "a-ha moment" surrounding that 25 percent cut in pay. When confronted with a loss in household revenue, you immediately began the process of DECIDING. The Bahamas, carpooling, Jennifer's ballet class—something has to go.

> The fact is, we are ALWAYS making economic decisions, whether we are conscious of this process or not. Unfortunately, whichever term you elect to work with, ignorance is not bliss. This chapter is not about making more money. It's about connecting the dots—applying economics to the decisions you make with the money you have.

A basic understanding of economics, coupled with a keen awareness of the role it plays in your everyday spending decisions, positions you to make choices that place you on a path to a good quality of life. To fulfill our goals in life, we often must make decisions about what to give up because of limited means. If we remove the financial constraint of economics, the only components that remain are time and how to spend it. This will allow us to choose a life that is led by the desires of our hearts, where we can move as a vessel to make lasting changes. When you firmly grasp and apply these concepts, you will make choices that are consistent with your personal and professional objectives and find alignment between the two.

How the Economy Works

Let's begin by recognizing and respecting the relationship between economics and money—they are first cousins. You cannot have one without the other. What you DON'T know about their relationship can derail your financial landscape, and thereby profoundly impact the quality of your life.

Economics is the study of how various entities allocate goods, services, and resources to fulfill the goal of ultimate satisfaction. That means that economics happens. Here's a simplified model: banks borrow money from the Federal Reserve Bank (FRB). Large corporations borrow money from banks at commercial rates. Large firms then employ people like you and me to develop, make, and sell goods and services. These companies disperse checks to employees. Employees then return what they earn to the economy by buying retail goods and services. Companies and employees both pay taxes on the money they have made to the Internal Revenue Service. The Federal Government then establishes a budget to pay for various expenditures, such as goods and services, and subsidy programs to disadvantage citizens.

The FRB manages the supply of money through loans to banks, regulations to banks, buying and selling of bonds to banks and the public, and through the interest rate. The interest rate then helps to gauge business and consumer consumption habits on interest-sensitive items.

An illustration of how the economy works is shown in the chart below:

The Circular Flow Diagram

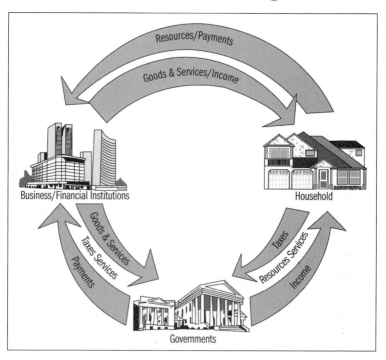

Who's in Charge Here?

You are a mini-economy. You work, receive a paycheck, and participate in economic activities on a daily basis. You are on a long-range journey of nothing but decisions, and you are running an economic marathon. You conduct economic activity in several ways: managing your revenue (paycheck), budgeting, managing your cash flow, and acquiring debt. All economic environments comprise these four important elements. Now start picturing yourself as the head of your economy.

The Economic Basics:
Revenue, Budgeting, Cash Flow, and Acquired Debt

Revenue

The amount of money you make is a choice. It is totally up to you how much money you want to extract from the economy. You can choose to make $15,000 a year or you can choose to make $15 million. You are the only person who can determine how much you make. Of course, the choice of how much money you make is directly related to the profession that you choose.

Let's examine this concept. Say you see someone on television playing tennis and you decide to become a professional tennis player. For the sake of our example, you are not seven years old, like you would have to be in real life; in fact, let's pretend you can become a professional tennis player as a young adult. So, you go out and begin to take lessons, and you love the game. You practice every day with the professional you hired at the local court. However, he says that you are a tremendous talent, and that he does not have the capability to give you what you need to make it to the professional tennis circuit. He instead refers you to someone who specializes in taking people from intermediate to professional. This example may lack realism, but the point is that you can start out in one place, and through a combination of passion and hard work, you can figure out how to get to your destination. Now in this case, it would probably be better to examine all options available to you in the beginning. In fact, the time spent with the first tennis coach may have hurt your chance to better yourself in the game that you love. My suggestion to you is:

> As soon as you decide what you want to do, sit down and gather all of the information available to you on the topic.

> Figure out the plausibility of your plan.

> If the journey appears achievable, map out your path.

> Determine all of the resources you require.

> Get to work!

Making the Right Decisions

Getting to the income level of your choice is very much like the tennis example. At any point in your life, you are able to decide how much money you want to make. You are able to go for it. Unfortunately, with tennis, you would have to be very young in order to have a chance at becoming a professional and earning money. In the world of professional work, however, you can choose at any point what you want to be and how much money you want to make.

In my case, I decided when I was 25 years old that

I wanted to earn $100,000 by the time I was 30. This was more than anyone in my immediate family earned currently or previous to that time. I did not care—all I knew was that my mother kept saying to me as a child, "You should be a doctor." What she didn't know was that I could not stand the sight of blood. In fact, I had a really hard time being around sick people. However, she added to that advice by constantly telling me I could be anything I wanted to be, and that was advice that I could do something with.

This $100,000 seemed to make sense as a revenue target. It did not come out of thin air. I was able to arrive at this number because of people I knew—I was able to take their experiences and then determine what I wanted to do that might somehow be able to use this new information.

You Can Choose Your Revenue

As a child, my idea of how to earn income was first to find out from my friends who was hiring. I would then complete a job application and hope the job paid well. This course of action was obviously not the way to control revenue. The point is that there are many approaches. I am not saying which one is right or wrong, only that you have a choice in what you do, and in the income derived from that choice.

You manage your revenue. Revenue is all of the dollars you earn from all sources. Most Americans have only two sources of revenue—a paycheck from an employer and a tax return from the federal or state government. Okay, so what is there to manage? First, you can make as much money as you want. This is a decision point for you and your family. The money you make is directly related to the quality of life you decide you want to have. I suggest that the earlier in life you make this decision the better, because it often requires an investment of years in order to achieve the objectives you desire. We will revisit this concept again in Chapter 6.

For now, let's look at sources of revenue. You have many options to determine from where you will derive your income. The reason most people receive their revenue from an employer is because it simplifies society. Imagine if every person represented an individual company and wanted to be in business on their own. This would present chaos for any national economy.

Let's reflect for a moment on the formation of a country. There are, say, 12 wise men and women sitting around a table. They have to decide how to get average people to work and at the same time allow them to have the basic necessities, such as food and shelter. One option might be to have each of them incorporate into their own company and engage each of them in a contract. The other option would be to have one of the people sitting at the table go out and gather the people, negotiate with them, and offer their services to the economy and at the same time, make a small profit. Now one person who was sitting at the table would be running a business, and his or her business would benefit society.

You must decide how close you want to be to the economy. Remember, a company is supposed to be a buffer for you from the uncertainties of the economy. A company evens out its cash flow and its management team should be smart enough to provide a somewhat focused charter. This is where you should judge them. You should seek a company with an economic strategy that you can believe in. Ask hard questions. Your employment choice is a vote of confidence in their management team.

As for your revenue, you may not sit at the management table, but the way you receive revenue, a paycheck, or whatever you might call it is a decision you must take seriously. You must decide upon the best option for your family. I do not advocate working a part-time job as a source of additional revenue. This may seem to be a quick fix to a short-term requirement; however, it does not leverage the investment you make eight hours a day. If you need additional income, it is much more desirable to figure out how to leverage the experience and training that you have on your regular job. You will command a higher hourly rate, and this would have less of an adverse impact on your family.

No matter how much money you have, you can still manage it. The important elements of revenue are, of course, the amount and when you get it. I am an advocate of using large payments to your advantage. Whether these payments represent a $500 tax return every year or a $5,000 commission check once a month, these payments should be treated as regular income and considered in your cash flow and budget.

Budgeting

This is where realism is applied to your plan. The idea here is to create a financial strategy and live by it. The corporate approach can provide a really good template for managing a budget. As we discussed earlier, I think it is important to take your family's financial objectives as seriously as any CEO of a corporation like IBM would. When I was working as a CEO, budgeting was one of my favorite areas. It was an opportunity to marry what we did for our customers (our projects) with the money we expected to receive (revenue and profits). It is your opportunity to do the same. Apply financial realism to your life plan by putting numbers on paper so you can see clearly how events will occur. You can plot out both milestones and major accomplishments.

The first component of your budget is revenue. As we discussed above, it is all of your dollars earned from all sources.

The second component is expenses. Although revenue is important, uncontrolled expenses can derail a well-intended budget. The intent here is to take your life plan, which you will develop later, and make good decisions on needs and wants. There is no way you can have everything. There are a handful people in the world who do not have to be concerned about placing limits on their spending, but most of the rest of us— and I mean 99.999999999 percent—have to place some limits on spending and live within our means. I suggest that you make these decisions as a family and make them consistent with the priorities in your life plan. This is an extremely important area, and you can lose control quickly. Whether you have $1,000 in savings or $1 million, you cannot spend without control, and there are things you just cannot afford.

Just as the revenue you earn is a choice, so is your level of spending. We will talk a great deal about a concept called "consumption orientation" in the next chapter. For now, I simply would like you to think about what makes sense for you and your family to spend. This decision should be made with your family's objectives in mind, and please ignore all of the signals sent to you by society. You do not have to drive a European sports sedan. You do not have to pay $200 for a pair of shoes. These things may mean nothing to you, or you may be cursing me for treading on your toes. I am not judging you for what you choose to buy or not to buy. I am, however, suggesting that you have a choice in everything you do, and that there are ripple effects to every decision. We will talk about this topic a great deal in the next chapter. So let's make good decisions and employ spending habits that allow us to accomplish our family's objectives.

Profit is the last item of our budget. This is the money left over from our revenue after we have concluded our spending for the month.

Cash Flow

This area deals with cash management decisions. Again, it is a good idea to use the corporation example, where we receive revenue from the sale of our services or merchandise. This is not very far-fetched, because our location on the chart we looked at before, describing the flow of goods and services, determines our source of revenue. We must think of ourselves as financial entities that get X amount of dollars a year and figure out how to deploy those dollars in the most effective ways, either monthly or in whatever time interval makes the most sense. This is an area that can be challenging for many people because we tend to feel powerless with respect to when and how we get our money, and when and how we have to pay it out.

First, it is important to manage when and how we pay our taxes. This is a major chunk of our cash flow. The U.S. government gives us the ability to decide how much comes out of each of our paychecks—this is done on the form W-4. There is no benefit to getting money back at the end of the year, unless we want to keep that money in a no-interest savings account that we could use to make a large expenditure.

Second, use healthy debt. A charge card (not a credit card) that you have to pay off at the end of each month is a good way to manage your spending because you receive a summary each month that tells you what you spent and where. There are other forms of debt that can help, which we will discuss shortly.

Again, remember that this is your money, and you decide when you should get it and when you should spend it. Not having cash available is simply a matter of a couple possibilities. You spend more than you make each month, or your expenditures are not timed to give you the cash flow you need to live daily. Managing your cash flow is an activity that will help you become comfortable with your financial life. Doing this well creates an environment where you can live within your budget and minimize the stress you feel around money issues.

Debt and How to Use It

Debt can be either your best friend or your worst enemy—and most of us are familiar with the worst enemy part. Good debt is used to accomplish short or long-term objectives. It is planned, and it allows us to have access to additional capital at favorable interest rates. Bad debt can be summarized as paying large amounts of interest on items without any thought behind the act. Unfortunately, no one gives us a handbook on how to manage or use debt until it is possibly too late. Then they are trying to teach us how not to make the same mistakes again. I will share with you my mistakes and successes.

Why Debt Exists

Debt is a necessary part of our global economy. In the United States, our economic cycle begins by major banks borrowing from the Federal Reserve. The terms of the debt allow the banks to loan money to corporations, as well as to you and me, and still make a profit. They borrow at an interest rate lower than the one they offer us. Large borrowers get better interest rates than you and I get as consumers.

As consumers, we are offered all kinds of opportunities to borrow money. We can borrow at our local department store or even our nearby furniture store. If we are creditworthy, we can keep the furniture for a year or more without paying for it. We do live in a great world, don't we? So what's the catch, since there is always that fine print?

In the case of the department store, their credit card division is a profit center. While it is wonderful that these credit cards allow stores to sell more merchandise, they make additional profit off of the 21 percent interest they charge you for the right to hold onto their money. For example, let's say you buy a leather coat for $300 at the Acme Department Store and put it on your Acme Credit Card. Your cash flow is not very good, so you pay the minimum payments of $10 a month for 2 years. If you continue with this course of action, you could soon pay $300 in interest and still have to pay the $300 in principle to buy the jacket that does not fit so well anymore.

I suppose store credit cards can be convenient in some occasions, but I can think of no reason to pay 21 percent interest for any purchase. Please manage your cash flow to avoid this kind of an expense at all costs. This is just giving away hard-earned money.

As for the furniture, you can keep it for a year or more without paying for it. This is a tempting proposition. In most cases, the interest accrues during a period of deferred payments, and if you pay the balance by the end of the deferral period, you get to use their money free for a year or more. GREAT DEAL, but only if you pay the debt off on time. Otherwise, I am sure that interest rate is above 20 percent, and paying this kind of interest will sting—again, you're giving away hard-earned money.

There are some cases where debt can be used to accomplish some tactical or strategic financial objectives. If neither of these objectives is a part of your decision, then it is probably bad debt.

Debt That Works For You

Enough talk about how not to use debt. What is good debt? This is the fun part. We did talk about one good way to use debt when describing the furniture purchase. If you can use someone else's money for one year without paying interest, that is very good debt. However, it is very important that you pay the debt before you have to pay any interest. Another great way to use debt is to buy a home. It is the only good deduction we can claim on our taxes today without owning a business. Let's describe a couple of ways corporations use debt to increase their profits. One popular way is a line of credit. This financial instrument allows the corporation to borrow money on an as-needed basis or when cash flow is tight. When they do happen to borrow against their line of credit, it is at a very good interest rate. For example, a good interest rate on a line of credit is 3 to 5 percent, which is a lot better than 21 percent, right? This rate, of course, depends on the current economic climate and the rate at which the Federal Reserve lends money to banks. When cash flow improves, typically within a month, the debt is repaid with the incoming cash. This is a way corporations smooth out their cash flow. Imagine expecting to get a paycheck from your company and they say payroll won't happen this week because cash flow is tight. Or, they say they are going to pay every other person, alphabetically. A line of credit is a much-needed financial instrument when companies are not cash-rich.

Another way corporations borrow money is through the use of term loans. These are simply loans for a specific need. For example, if a corporation wants to invest $100,000 in a project with a projected return of 40 percent on its investment, the corporation could then borrow the $100,000 and pay it back over the life of the project. Of course, the interest rate would be favorable at say 5 or 6 percent. This of course produces a 35 or 34 percent profit on the money borrowed. This is the way we should think about using debt. How can

I as a consumer use debt tactically or strategically to improve the quality of life for my family?

Keep Your Debt Healthy

Now let's provide some examples of good ways to use consumer debt. Healthy debt is a very important part of a good economy. You practice healthy debt when you borrow money from banks at a lower percentage rate than you earn it. As mentioned earlier, purchasing a home is an example of healthy debt. If you borrow the money to purchase a home at 6 percent interest, and the home value appreciates at 7 percent, your net income is the 1 percent difference, plus the dollars you saved by deducting the interest from your taxes due. You acquired good debt because you made more than you paid. This would be an example of a healthy term loan.

If you happen to work on commission and your income has been the same every year or has gone up consistently, and you are confident of how much you will make each year, you are a good candidate for a line of credit strategy. This can be as simple as using a low-interest credit card to balance your cash flow. In this circumstance, you can calculate your monthly fixed expenses, which are simply the expenses you have to pay each and every month. Just because your income may vary from month to month and you are very confident about what you will make for the whole year, there is no need to panic. This is a good instance to use your low-interest credit card or line of credit on your home to pay off your expenses for the current or next month. The important part of this example is that at the end of the year, the interest payments you have made allowed you to smooth out your cash flow and allowed you and your family to work in an environment that rewards you with commissions for your hard work.

There Are Always Opportunities

My experience with debt did not start off very good. After graduating from high school and landing a job at Penney's, I bought a new car and signed up for payments for four years. At the age of 19, I was making what was considered *good money*; I also discovered Mr. MasterCard and Ms. Visa. While attempting to attend college at night, I soon discovered that I had to quit school because I had to meet my debt obligations and could not afford to pay tuition. I knew I did not want to see this hand play out totally. It seemed I would be anchored to a job that had no future all because I acquired unhealthy debt.

I opted to make a drastic move and enlist in the Air Force, where I could restructure my debt and continue my education. I am not advocating military service. I am, however, suggesting that you do not acquire unhealthy debt at all. But if you do make mistakes, it is not the end of the world. Do not give up on your future. There are always options to restructure your obligations in order to advance your vision of your future.

Exercises

1. Do a budget on a single piece of paper. Just jot down
   the following:

> > How much you expect to make over the next 12 months?
> > Breaking this down to a monthly amount is manageable.

> > What are your monthly fixed expenses? Include everything
> > you pay each and every month, such as mortgage/rent,
> > utilities, car payment, insurance, cable, telephone, pre-
> > scriptions, and so on. Some of these may be automatical-
> > ly deducted from your bank account.

> > What are your variable expenses? These occur throughout
> > the course of the year, but their timing is not easily pre-
> > dictable. This is the area where most people get into trou-
> > ble, and is also most easy to adjust. These are the expens-
> > es you will exercise control over. Examples of variable
> > expenses include: restaurant bills, movie tickets, or rentals,
> > toys for your children, clothing, groceries, unexpected home
> > or auto repairs, gifts, or any other expenses that cannot be
> > anticipated. Note: When you go to a store, make a list, and
> > try not to deviate from your objectives. Try to avoid impulse
> > purchases. This can be a real trouble spot when attempting
> > to follow a budget!

> > If you do not own a program like Quicken or Microsoft
> > Money that allows you to track your income and expenses,
> > buy one now! Do not fear. Most software is beginner-
> > friendly and includes an online tutorial. These companies
> > also provide phone support. If you need help with this
> > part, please get it. It is very important to track your income
> > and spending.

> > Do a profit and loss statement at the end of each month.
> > This is easy to do within a program like Quicken or
> > Microsoft Money. You can now see if you are spending more
> > than you make.

2. Evaluate your debt at the end of each year to determine if it is structured in a healthy way. This as an opportunity to use the healthiest forms of debt possible. Keep in mind that the healthiest form of debt is a low-interest rate loan that is tax-deductible. This kind of a loan includes a mortgage on your home and often a second mortgage. The worst form of debt is high-interest, revolving credit, such as a credit card. This is an exercise that corporations use to help to improve cash flow, so why can't you?

Sample Budget Form

	BUDGETED		ACTUAL	
	Annual Income	Monthly Income	Annual Income	Monthly Income
	$40,000	$3,333		
Fixed Expenses				
Federal Tax				
State Tax				
Other Tax				
Rent/Mortgage				
Car Payment				
Insurance				
Cable				
Telephone				
Medical Expenses				
Variable Expenses				
Restaurants				
Cleaners				
Movie Tickets				
Miscellaneous				
Remainder				

CHAPTER 2
CONSUMPTION ORIENTATION

I'm tired of hearing about money, money, money, money, money. I just want to play the game, drink Pepsi, and wear Reebok.

—Shaquille O'Neal

Spending Without Thought

Along my life journey, I met a man who had a profound impact on me, and I dedicate this chapter him. I do not know if he made up the term "consumption orientation," but I have never forgotten the concept. Tim, this is for you.

The man I am referring to used to be my customer. He and I spoke about matters close to both of our hearts. We both happened to work in an environment that valued intellect above most other things. It was a government laboratory, and my job was to sell computer systems and services; one of his jobs was to buy them. I have no hesitation in calling Tim my friend for life. We share spiritual values that I am sure will never change in either of us.

One day Tim invited me to his home, and during the visit, he seemed to feel almost obligated to explain his rationale for living where he did. I listened intently as he told me the reason he lived in a roughly 1,800 square foot home in a particularly nice neighborhood. It was because he chose not to be a blind consumer. He chose not to embrace consumption orientation. He told me his choices were a reflection of his wish to value his family. Additionally, his choice to work for the government allowed him to come home at a reasonable hour each day, to spend time with his wife and children.

This was a lot for me to digest, and I had many questions. I had never heard anything quite like this before. He was making choices in areas where people tended to just go along with whatever program seemed to make sense at the time. Congratulations, Tim, for having this kind of courage.

Tim had two children. His home, the car he drove, the fact that he wore the same clothes a couple times a week all allowed his children to be home-schooled and spend time absorbing the values of his choosing, versus those of the world. He explained that these were choices, and he would not embrace the values of the world because they did not work for his family. As I looked around his neighborhood, I saw that most people had larger homes and newer, bigger cars. Tim made choices counter to his apparent environmental culture. I cannot tell you what gave him the courage to make those choices, but his story should provide motivation to those who say they can't afford to do this or that, or they have to work late and cannot make Jennifer's piano recital or little Joey's soccer game.

What is important to you? Do you realize that anything important is in fact a choice? Your life should be a project that incorporates all of the values you want to express. It should reflect what is important to you; you only get one shot to get life right.

What Is Really Important

I would like to recall an experience with you. I remember it as if it just happened—the moment my daughter came into this world. On the day she was born, I remember feeling a bit shocked by the experience. I really did not know what to think. I felt inadequate and not sure of how to measure up to the task of being a parent. The feeling that stuck with me most, however, came from when I held my baby for the first time. I knew love for my parents, for other family members, and how it felt to love a wife. This was different. Now it felt like all of my love lived outside of my heart. I mean that this little person had my heart and everything she experienced—both good and bad—I would feel! The thought was overwhelming.

I have since adjusted to this feeling. Being a parent is the best thing I have ever experienced on this earth, and it is by far the most rewarding and best part of my life. A part of my feeling of inadequacy came from wondering if I could get this parenting thing right. It is absolutely something you have to learn about every day of your life. You have to be willing to admit to your shortcomings and be committed to using everything you learn to help you be a better parent. When I look at my daughter, I know she did not ask to come into this world. I believe I owe her my best effort in all aspects of life. I knew I had to have the courage to embrace the best practices of parenting and change in any way necessary. Are you ready to change for your current family or family to be? Are you ready to be your best self?

Consumption orientation is in direct competition with good parenting. It forces us to allow society to establish the values for our household. Economics is a strong force in life. Money helps to control our circumstances. Financial stress is a force that places a significant amount of pressure on a family. It is real, and it causes families to live in ways that relieve the pressure caused by excessive commitments such as by working extra hours to pay for things that bring no extra value to the family. What is all of this stuff about? It is all about your decisions.

The world has several paths laid out for us and all we have to do is pick ours. Let's talk about some that are available to us. Advertisers pick people they think we find interesting in a way that would make us want to emulate them. These people are popular enough to have a public brand—when you think about that person, you think of what they stand for. I will cite some examples to which you probably can relate.

Are you the Lenny Kravitz type, where staying in shape is a top priority? You must have the latest jeans, you want to appear to be in style; you must have a convertible and wear clothes from the Gap. Or are you more the Pierce Brosnan character—smooth, stylish, wearing the latest expensive chronograph from Breitling? Your hair, of course, has to be perfect.

And then there are Sarah Jessica Parker, Queen

Latifah, Tiger Woods, Jennifer Lopez, Hugh Grant, Halle Berry, Michael Jordan, and the newly on the scene Dwayne Wade, Carmelo Anthony or Serena Williams. Who gets your attention? All of these people are paid to sell you different products. I am not suggesting that we consciously attempt to emulate them. Is there, however, a collage of their personality traits in our minds, or do we consciously focus on a few characters we find worthy of our attention? These are topics worthy of some thought. We do get our senses of style and desire from somewhere. They do not come from thin air. No matter how strong we are, the media is a factor in our lives and the images have a powerful effect on us, whether conscious or not. One thing I can tell you for sure is that advertisers do not want you to pay too much attention to this concept, or else the dollars they spend for celebrities to endorse their products will be a total waste.

Every Action You Take
Is the Result of a Decision You Make

Now that we know advertisers need us at least to consider the people they put in front of us, what are we going to do? We need to make decisions that are consistent with our objectives, PERIOD. Everything you do is the result of a decision you make. To understand this concept is truly to begin to take control of your life and of course, the quality of the life you lead. This chapter is about economics, but I am sure you can see other applications of this concept in your life. Let's continue to talk about consumption orientation.

If you believe your purpose in life is to work all the

time, and that is the only source of joy in your life, then this chapter is not for you. However, if you know somewhere in the back of your mind that your joy is derived from your relationships, then we have something to talk about. I am in no way saying your life does not or cannot have meaning if you do not desire to be a parent. I am suggesting that all joy is in some way tied to our desire to spend time with other human beings. I would bet you that if you were given all of the desires of your heart today, every one of your wishes would involve someone you care for. If we examine our favorite activities, such as going to dinner, traveling, or even working or playing sports, we would find that most of these activities involve other people. Imagine the vacation of our dreams alone! We are not made to be alone. We are made to desire the company of the people we love. This is normal.

As I reflect on my life and the things I have accomplished in business, I have come to realize what is truly important to me. I do not want to do things very often unless they involve a loved one. A vacation is not truly a vacation without someone to enjoy it with. Going to a special restaurant is not the same without someone you care about to share the meal with. Let's face it, we need people in our lives to complete us. Of course, we are capable of living life alone, but other people make our experiences really special and meaningful.

Our choices of style and who we want to emulate has a great deal of influence on our quality of life. Let's say you've graduated from college and you have been in the workforce for three years. You are a lawyer and making a handsome salary of $120,000 a year. Through a combination of the images you have in your head, you decide you deserve a loft apartment that costs you $5,000 a month. Additionally, you need that Mercedes convertible which costs another $1,000 a month. Of course, you have to shop at Saks Fifth Avenue, so your wardrobe adds at least another $500 a month. Once we add the expense of going out to dinner several times a week and the various happy hours you attend, what might have been a comfortable salary is now a struggle.

It All Adds Up

There are many ways to practice consumption orientation. You do not have to be a lawyer and you do not have to live in a city in a loft apartment or even shop at Saks. What is your situation and what are the choices you make? Do you have objectives? The example I gave involves a single person. Now let's give this person a family, a spouse and two children. Do people make these kinds of choices when they have the responsibility of a family? Of course they do. Let's look at a family consisting of two college-educated adults who were recently married and are now enjoying the luxury of two incomes. What do they do? With their combined income of $150,000 they buy a $500,000 home in the suburbs and two or three cars, and they both dress in the latest styles. And on and on and on and on…Struggling? Yes they are!

Those kinds of choices may occur after getting a post-college job or at any point where there is progression in life, such as a promotion. We tend to take on some debt to support our new appetites because we know we have jobs to support our desires. Interest is not such a bad thing, is it? Though often, we do not understand the full impact of the credit agreements we are signing.

From this point, we typically buy things until we maximize our income and if we are really good, we have a little bit to save. These purchases can include a house, clothes, a car, and anything else that supports our lifestyle, which can lead to a very unhealthy existence. It can and often does lead to a life that involves a detrimental level of debt. You do not get enough rest because you are making a long commute or working long hours. You spend much of your time trying to figure out how to pay your bills or buy the next thing that you probably do not really need. Additionally, you look in your closet and you have stuff you don't even want or like. Even though life is tough financially, you still find time to shop and figure out if there is something you can buy just to pick up your mood. Of course, this is just one possible scenario, but it is real. Please remember all of these are decision points. Life can be very different depending upon the decisions you make.

An alternative approach might look something like this. You know who you value and how and where you want to spend your time, so you can pick a job that allows you to live according to these priorities. Choosing an occupation with a simple commute must be a high priority. Additionally, you must allow enough time to have dinner with your loved ones if not every day, then close to it. You must take adequate vacations to see family or friends at least once a year. Come up with a budget that allows you to advance your objectives. Pick a style that allows you to live the life that is important to you and your family. Does this sound too good to be true? Remember, life is about choices. When we discuss your life plan, you will see how to put these choices into action. You can enjoy your life!

The Cumulative Effect

Are the choices mentioned bad in and of themselves? Of course not. Is it bad to want the finer things in life? NO! You have one life, and I suggest you make choices that allow you to enjoy it to the fullest. I am attempting simply to help you wrap your priorities around all of the decisions you have to make and to achieve the balance that will allow you to enjoy this life as much as possible. Economic decisions can be a joy one day and true pain the next, and this shift can occur before you know it. Living and consuming without careful thought can dig a hole for you quickly. What are your priorities? Are you preparing for the life you really want to have? Do you already have your family? How do these decisions impact your ability to parent?

If you practice consumption orientation, there will be an impact on your family. You may not see a direct result from a single purchase, but you will see the cumulative effect. Once you purchase something you cannot afford, there is a bill you cannot pay comfortably. This bill requires you pay it over a longer time than you should. As we all know, bills do not come by themselves. Once you start on this road, it is difficult to get off. So now we have to figure out how not to pay something else or eliminate this bill or make more money right away. As you can see, this is not an easy scenario to deal with. Ultimately it is difficult to be the best person you can be while dealing with this kind of economic bondage and working as many hours as possible in order to dig out. Let's make good, long-term decisions with the knowledge in mind that no decisions are free.

Let's Talk About Our Strategy

In order to have a really good life we must understand and embrace the concept of strategic thinking and aggressively apply it to our lives. Strategic thinking involves developing tactics around a central life theme. No matter how many years we have lived thus far, it is not too late to implement this approach. First you must decide who is most important to you, who you want to spend the most time with, and what is really important about these relationships. Then you simply have to build a life strategy around these people.

Let's say your close circle includes one child, a significant other, and a parent who is approaching their twilight years. You then decide what kind of priorities you want to wrap around these people. What kind of time do you want to be able to spend with them? What is important in their lives and how can you positively impact them? How does all of this impact you? What do you want out of your life? Now you are ready to think about your career and the types of economic decisions you need to make. These are the people who will truly impact your quality of life. In Chapters 4, 5 and 6, you will build a life plan around these values.

This life plan should be based on the best practices available without the boundaries of your current economic scenario. Instead of reinventing the wheel, select the qualities and habits to the best of your ability and use them as tools to navigate your decisions. This plan should match your value system. For example, when purchasing a car, you should select one that fits within your budget and does not negatively impact your cash flow. This principle of applying best practices works in other areas as well. Find someone who has already achieved what you want, and emulate them. Keep focused on what is easily affordable and what fits in with your family's priorities.

When entering marriage, it would be good to discuss the nuts and bolts, such as whether you both want children and if so, how important it is for one parent to stay home with the little people. Decide your stylistic selection—do you have to shop at Saks or can you get by with J.C. Penney or Target? These questions should be considered prior to jumping into a lifestyle aimed at lining the pockets of big advertisers and retailers.

Write down all your plans and match them with your priorities. Where you work, for example, should be a line item in your family's life plan. This may help curtail the number of marital problems caused by arguments about money.

Scratch the idea of paying bills. Many of us have been socialized to believe that bills automatically accompany purchases. When you eliminate the consumption orientation lifestyle, you don't accumulate bills—you pay cash or use a charge card that requires you to pay off the balance at the end of each month, or you can use other healthy forms of debt.

Take a Good Look at Your Motives

All decisions begin with a thought; it's the quality of that thought that leads to good decisions, which ultimately yield good results. Unfortunately, some of us are more at ease with a familiar, bad decision than an unfamiliar, sound one. Let's shift the thinking AWAY from economics as a faraway concept and into the mindset of economics as decisions you make every day.

By virtue of having objectives and your willingness to make hard decisions, you are going against the grain in this life. Again, I cannot overstate that society does not expect you to see these areas as decision points. We spoke earlier in this chapter about making life decisions around an unhealthy lifestyle. This can get you into trouble quickly.

Consumption orientation is just a choice. You can live anyway you choose. You can spend time with those who are important to you. You can truly experience joy. Just remember to choose well. Did this decision make good sense? Are you at the agonizing stage Confucius so aptly predicted when you don't economize?

This chapter on consumption orientation challenges you to dig deeper, to step outside your familiar zone of financial discomfort. I want you to scrutinize your spending habits with simple questions such as, "What am I buying here and why?" "How will this decision affect me, my family, and my life?" Simply put, does this decision make sense? You'd be surprised how you would spend your money if these questions were answered before you decided to buy.

When you examine your thinking about what you consume—not the actual purchase—and your motives for doing so, you're on your way to conquering consumption orientation.

Fruit Doesn't Fall Far From the Tree

So where did we get our thinking about spending?

In the mid-1990's, a line in the song "I Believe I Can Fly" by R. Kelly became the mantra for many high school and college graduates: "If you can see it, then you can be it." Quoted by many commencement speakers, its purpose was to impart the importance of reaching toward a higher plane in life. It also implied that our achievements are only limited by our imagination.

Most of us have already established our views on spending way before high school or college, so we can logically conclude they began at home, passed on to us by our parents. This has nothing to do with a person's ability to parent. Whether parents possess economic savvy or not, they seldom show their children the connection between spending habits and life priorities.

Lack of discussion in this arena is matched equally by the child's total lack of interest in the subject. Do you know any children begging their parents to teach them how to pay bills? Here lies the paradox—the total annihilation of the subject of responsible spending. By not teaching our children about spending and priorities, we are unknowingly making a decision to teach them that such decisions don't matter.

Usually, little thought is given to the impact all this decision-making will have on the quality of life. For example, let's look at another important area—the choice of a career. You decide that you want to be a lawyer based solely on the six-figure income it could yield, or because you want to be of service to people. This will allow you to buy that coveted home in suburbia. For many, career analysis typically ends with the dreams of the house. However, you failed to think it through to determine if you TRULY prefer working 80 hours a week or prefer to enjoy dinner with your family every night.

This decision established what was important to you at the time. You decided to become a lawyer and work many late hours rather than come home at five p.m., hang out with the wife and kids, and go to bed at a reasonable hour. You never asked if such a decision would ultimately prevent you from having a close relationship with your children and eventually grandchildren. You didn't stop to think, *Which is more important—the big house or my children?*

This scenario is not designed to imply that law is a bad career decision. What's important is how that decision will impact what is truly important to you.

Conquering consumption orientation, simply put, means that you have to first assess what you do and why you do it. Next, you have to focus on making good decisions. Both of these are components of the life plan that we will complete later in our journey together.

Exercises

1. Now that you have a program like Quicken or Microsoft Money and you've entered all your expenditures, you can see each and every transaction. Look at each dollar spent and determine if they are in line with your family's objectives. An objective could be to spend some good, quality time as a couple or family, so let's not be too hard on ourselves.

2. Cut the expenses that are not healthy! How are you blowing your budget? Do you spend too much on impulse purchases when you go to the department store? Or is your challenge the grocery store—or maybe the movies or restaurants? Remember, the easiest expenses to control are the ones that are variable. Examine them closely and remember that this exercise is to keep us on track, to achieve our overall objectives, and maintain a good quality of life!

3. Decide what you and your family need for a healthy, complete existence. Make healthy choices!

4. Remember, good discipline must accompany rewards. Delayed gratification is okay but should not be overdone. Do not spend unwisely, but enjoy life and your loved ones. Do not confine yourself to a diet of beans and rice every day unless you are in real financial difficulty! Include a vacation to one of your favorite destinations in your budget and put money aside to save for it. Preplan so that you do not feel pressure to finance this kind of expenditure with credit cards that you cannot afford to pay off at the end of the month.

THE SWINE AND THE BIRD

One day, a sparrow flies into a stinking piggery, where she watches a swine gobble down his food.

Seeing his unexpected visitor, the swine starts boasting about his life. "I live like a king here. I don't even have to lift a paw to get something to eat. Several times a day, someone comes to bring me food. I do nothing but eat and sleep—what a life!"

The little bird says nothing."

"How you must envy me," says the swine as he fills his mouth with swill.

"It is you who must be envious of me," trills the sparrow.

"I envy you? Never!" protests the swine loudly. "I am like a king in this pen while you have to work for your food. You are a slave to your needs!"

At this the sparrow flies away, leaving the swine munching his meal noisily.

After some time, the sparrow returns to the piggery. Piercing screams are coming from the pen. Flying nearer, she sees the plump swine being led to a nearby slaughterhouse.

The swine looks up and sees the sparrow. While he strains against the rope that binds him, the swine tells the little bird, "I lived like a king and now I shall die like a slave."

After uttering these words, the swine sees the butcher sharpening his knife as he follows the flight of the sparrow with envious eyes.

The best lessons we can learn are those that do not come from our own painful experience. If someone attempts to share wisdom with you, listen and make sure you understand what they are saying! Put your pride aside! Others may have our best interests at heart and they may see that life is about to deal us a cruel blow. Don't be like the swine in our example. If your life seems like it's too good to be true and you don't have to put in any effort for your quality of life, then it probably is too good to be true. Keep your eyes open.

CHAPTER 3
CULTURAL CONTEXT

"How do you start to write a play, Mr. Williams?"
"I start," he said sharply, "with a sentence."

—Gore Vidal,
on playwright Tennessee Williams

Remember Joey, the kid next door who practiced playing his trumpet ALL the time? Every Saturday morning, before the first lawnmower jumped, you heard Joey. Sunday evening, while sneaking in that last snooze, there was Joey. During prayer, Joey. From sun-up to sun-down, Joey squealed his off-key lungs out, driving you totally nuts. You were just *waiting* for the day when you mustered up the nerve to shout, "Hey Joey! Stop! You cannot PLAY the trumpet Joey. You will NEVER be able to play, Joey. So give that trumpet and my sanity a rest, will you?!" You didn't know or care whether Joey was just learning to play the trumpet. You just wanted him to stop.

Years later, while half-asleep and listening to late-night television, you mused at what you thought was "Heeerreee's Johnny!" *Hmmm*, you thought. *When did Johnny Carson reruns begin?* Only it wasn't Johnny—it was Joey. Heeerrreee's Joey! He was racking up a host of awards on late-night TV for mastering the toughest

Miles Davis pieces ever played—one squeal at a time—
and making millions.

Perhaps you don't know anyone who stumbled
along and made it big. But what small beginnings and
big endings are etched in your mind? Like the look on
your child's face the day he took his first step without
holding your hand?

It All Begins With Our Cultural Contexts

We all have beginnings, but they are not all the same.
Because of our cultural contexts, we vary in our environments, upbringing, habits, and beliefs. Cultural
context is the blueprint you were handed to approach
life, the set of problem-solving tools that equip you
and guide your decisions. It's up to you to modify
your existing blueprint, start fresh with a new one
based on best practices you've witnessed, or employ a
combination of both to effect change.

In Chapter 2, we reviewed our spending conduct.
We looked at the futility of consumption orientation
and the deprived financial conditions it can create.
This chapter is meant to make you uncomfortable—
shifting the focus from conditions to causes. That
means going inside cultural context and perusing the
predecessor of our thinking.

Examining our cultural context is tough because the
knowledge we gain wipes out the excuse for change.
Change takes guts; only when we trudge through the
mazes of our cultural baggage are we better equipped
to evaluate and dispense of useless ideas that hamper
our purposes in life. Any less effort impedes the self-
actualization for which each of us was designed.

At the end of this chapter, I hope you will be closer to answering some tough questions about yourself. Why am I not where I want to be financially, physically, spiritually and emotionally? Could it be I never took stock of my baggage or saw its relationship to achievement? Perhaps I became a victim of the delusion that my starting point—my cultural context—always prescribed my end?

To get closer to the answers, we must stop playing ostrich. Let's take our heads out of the sand and try to discover what's really going on.

We will start where we left off in Chapter 2. Most of us inherited poor financial patterns from our parents. Consumption orientation led us to consume without thinking, compounding one bad spending decision upon another. Because no one showed us the consequences of spending without thinking, we thought it was okay.

However, it's *not* okay. Careful thought should precede all decisions relating to money. Consider the owner of the local delicatessen. Time is fast approaching for him to balance his year-end books, and it's not looking good. His shelves are lined with strudel some salesman convinced him would put his deli on the international map, only he was wrong—no one bought them. What storeowner wants to toss out shelves of unsold products? Leftover merchandise means money down the drain. There's only one way that deli owner can recover—he must first accept that his inventory is worthless. Without remorse, he must get rid of it to make room for items that sell. He must squarely face this loss, inventorying each strudel he throws out. But the final blow does not come when he swoons, "Bye

bye, strudel!" No, that comes when his books show red at the end of the year.

Self-examination is a process, not an event. The deli owner's process of recovery began when he took a look at those full shelves. Only then—when he *recognized* that he had an item that wouldn't sell, followed by guiltless resolution to let it go—could he hope for a more prosperous profit margin in the coming year. Permanent change is always preceded by honest self-examination.

Never Underestimate the Glory of Cultural Context

Cultural context is powerful. For example, if someone were asked to describe your character, values, or personality, what information would they use to formulate their answer? Would their perusal of you be predicated on your thoughts, words, or actions? Be mindful that while *we* often judge ourselves by our intentions, *others* evaluate us by what we say and do.

The fact is, each of us is merely a compilation of our thoughts and actions. It is not too far-fetched to assume, then, that much of our identities are prescribed by what we say and do. Cultural context is powerful because it influences *all* of your thoughts and actions, and anything that has the power to influence your thoughts and actions surely has the power to influence *you*.

Cultural context is neither good nor bad, but most good ideas are simple. Cultural context is everything. It has to do with the fact that we are male or female. We are White, Black, Italian, Jewish, Polish, Russian, Chinese, Hispanic, Indian, French, and so on. We are poor, we are wealthy. We emulate our parents, we rebel. We choose to take the path of least resistance and follow in established cultural footsteps, or we take risks and fall forward—*our* way. Cultural context fuses all these forces to influence how we think, what we say, and mostly, our decisions.

Not in My Backyard

Many people never prosper economically because they don't even know they *have a* cultural context. It's not the cultural context that holds them back—it's their inability to recognize it. This insidious phenomenon dominates almost every area of our lives. Refusal to see your own cultural context is similar to a blacksmith who goes out of business because horses keep stumbling in the shoes he's made. He assumes the shoes are damaged, but never thinks to sharpen his tools.

One way to understand your cultural context is to return to your hometown after a long hiatus. Anxious to catch up on old news, you drop by Uncle Petey's Tavern for one of those infamous Long Island iced teas. In walks Gloria—the high school homecoming queen every guy fantasized about. Back then, one of Gloria's most notable attributes was matching her eye shadow to every outfit she wore—green boots, green eye shadow. And from the attention she's getting at this moment, all the guys *still* think Gloria is hot.

Except you. Gloria is still beautiful, but you now prefer a more natural type of beauty. You're asking yourself, *Did I really think all that makeup was attractive?* Yes, you did. And had you stayed living in your hometown, you may have married Gloria. Not that I have anything against matching eye shadow with clothing or with women like Gloria, but you get the point.

Once you accept that there is a myriad of perceptions in this big wide world, limited only by your cultural experiences, then you can begin to notice your own cultural context.

Great Expectations—Does This Baggage Belong to You?

Expectations are formed through a combination of our environments and what we decide to do with the information we have received. For most of us, the environment is comprised of people in close proximity to us, such as parents, friends, and teachers. We further enlarge our cultural experiences as we enter the work world, marry, have children, and gain access to other worlds through the media. But these seldom have the impact of our parents.

This Is NOT Your Father's Oldsmobile!

According to most child development experts, your personality is pretty much set by the time you're six years old. So, who do you think got a hold of you before you expanded your world? The most precipitous but subtle cultural context comes from our parents.

Parents have the ability to project their cultural context onto their children. That's fine, except when this baggage comes in the form of low expectations and opposes higher ones you've set for yourself. The validity of parents' cultural context is seldom questioned but often mimicked, even when we don't wish to. It's like the abusive person who swore they would never be like their abusive parents, but looks in the mirror one day and sees Mom and Dad staring right back.

Let's examine how a parent's expectations can undermine a decision that falls outside their cultural guideposts. Say you've worked on a farm in America's dairy land—Pewaukee, Wisconsin—all your life. You have two loyal cows who you named Molly and Mo on the day they were born. You adore Molly and Mo, but the milk money they produce isn't sufficient to purchase that Mercedes you've longed for. How can you ever afford a fancy car when you've been, and are expected to continue, milking Molly and Mo all your life? For goodness' sake, YOU *need* a job delivering milk!

But guilt prevents you from leaving. Dad grew up on this farm and it's been passed down through six generations. Dad invested his life savings nurturing this land to support you and the rest of the family. He's proudly looking forward to the day he can pass you the baton of this great family institution. Simply put, your father realized his own self-actualization through the success of that farm. But then along came you at generation seven, upsetting the equilibrium with your desire to move to the city, get a job delivering milk, buy a Mercedes, and blow *his* entire life's dream to pieces.

The other side of the coin is growing up wealthy. You already HAVE a Mercedes, and so do your dad, mom, and friends. The sense of entitlement to luxury silently dictates that you'll buy several more Mercedes in your lifetime. Unknown to everyone around you is your deep yearning to scrap the Mercedes, live on a farm in Pewaukee, and write mystery novels to the soft mooing of cows at sunrise. Forget a Mercedes— how 'bout a pick up truck?

What's the common dilemma here? Molly and Mo, or a Mercedes? The unanimous prognosis of family and friends is that these children's *minds* are the dilemma—they've *lost* them.

However, the real problem is the parents' expectations. This may lead you to wonder, *Could they be right?* But the most evasive dilemma lies in the question you must ask yourself: *Could they be wrong?*

It hurts to let go of some things, especially the nod of acceptance we crave from those closest to us. You may not be able to distinguish that rejecting your parents' cultural context is not equivocal to rejecting *them*. Breaking away from generations of ideas which invalidate your aspirations, dreams, and talents is no easy task, particularly when those expectations impose a mediocrity you cannot live with peacefully. Yet there often is an inner drive that propels you to step out of the boundaries of cultural context. The failure, therefore, is not in your aspiration, but in the perceived need for the very acceptance that prevents you from cultivating your special gifts.

Your Vision—The Fight for YOUR Life

Henry Ford, who revolutionized America's *modus operandi* from agriculture to industrialism, faced a similar problem. Born in an era of farming, Ford was no stranger to tough work. He left his own family farm at 16 to work in a Detroit machine shop. The cultural context for most working Americans of that period was to work on a farm, live outside of the city, and travel by horse, because cars were too expensive for the average person.

But Ford had a vision. The first part of that vision was manufacturing. Instead of having workers assemble one car at a time, Ford had organized teams add parts to each Model T as it moved down the assembly line. By 1914, he had developed the world's first automatic conveyor belt that could churn out a car every 93 minutes. The second part of Ford's vision was to pay wages that would allow his workers to afford the Model T. His formula of mass-producing cars and making them affordable for everybody revolutionized America's way of doing business. His creation of the assembly line was the final push that ushered in America's Industrial Revolution.

Prior to Ford's development of the auto assembly line, coupled by his workers' ability to afford them, only two out of eight Americans lived in the cities. By World War II, that figure had doubled, all because of the affordable Model T.

Ford had been putting cars together since 1891, and he always had critics. The *Wall Street Journal* dubbed his vision "an economic crime," and "Fordism" was viewed scornfully by many. But Ford's continuous wage increase to $10 daily (the average before that was $2 to $3.30 a day) proved critical to making the automobile accessible to all. And his assembly line enabled him to cut the cost of each car. His profits skyrocketed as his workers both made and bought his Model Ts.

Thank heavens Ford ignored his critics and followed his own vision. Who knows what would have happened if he didn't? We might all be living on farms and traveling by horse.

Delusions of Grandeur—Thank God I'm Not THAT Bad

Ah, friends. You gotta love 'em. They validate, encourage, and accept you in spite of your quirky derelictions. Even when you change, your true friends remain. Like your parents, friends can deeply influence you. They differ from your parents in that they don't purposely attempt to carve out the map of your life. But they can, without malice, send out messages that the cultural context you were handed as a child is totally acceptable. In fact, it is highly likely that you and your close friends shared similar blueprints, which is why you became such good friends in the first place.

But what if your friends' ideas are entwined in a blueprint you've outgrown? What if your friends have never examined the issue of cultural context and are satisfied with a *status quo* that works for them, but not you? Or what if they have scrutinized their cultural baggage and chose not to alter it?

Friendships are a tricky form of cultural context—they can trick you into believing that "good" is as good as it gets, when what you want is the best. Take for instance your friend who is doing quite well. She got the MBA, earns six figures, and occupies a luxury suite in a ritzy downtown office. She's doing okay, but you earn $5,000 more than she does annually and your office has a bigger bathroom—so you MUST be doing better than okay.

The only problem is, you're not satisfied with occupying a penthouse—you want to OWN the building. Using your friends' standards as a barometer of your progress reinforces the same cookie-cutter limitations imposed on you by well-meaning parents.

Another way you can acquire cultural baggage through friendships is to follow the crowd. Take the kid who was teased all his life. To his surprise (and delight), he's no longer being bullied. There's a new kid in town who is now the target of merciless taunting. Having been bullied himself, this kid empathizes with the new kid's distress. Grateful that he's now been accepted, he joins his newfound friends in hurting the new kid. For the price of fitting in, he has already begun the habit of sacrificing his own principles.

These circumstances pose no real challenges to friendships, but they can pit you against yourself. When we debate our own instincts based on what other people say, we dilute the insight and energy needed to stay focused. Here, we learn there's some truth to the adage, "Stand for something or fall for anything." Instead of giving credence to doubt, you must trust your own positive inner spirit.

A more difficult challenge surrounding friendships and cultural context is when seeds of your new cultural context begin to bear fruit. We seldom lay claim to one of the oldest emotions known to mankind—envy. This is not to say that friends envy our accomplishments; in fact, they are usually our loudest cheerleaders. But that doesn't preclude them, or any human being, from feeling a tinge of jealousy at times. The worst response we can have to envy is continuously to downplay our new accomplishments or financial status because others are uncomfortable with it.

Am I My Brother's Keeper?

The first murder recorded in the Bible grew out of envy. The story of brothers Cain and Abel indicates that both presented gifts to God, who honored Abel's gift but rejected Cain's. Jealous of his brother's standing in the sight of God, Cain killed Abel. When God questioned Cain about Abel's whereabouts, Cain coined the phrase, "Am I my brother's keeper?" This is not designed to portray a morbid picture of friends' attitudes toward any newfound success. The point is that jealousy may come from a friend, even though you've been as close as brothers.

"Settling" for others' choices diminishes our creativity. Worse, it could lead to chronic discontent for years to come. Deep dissatisfaction is similar to road rage—unprocessed anger that seemingly pops up from nowhere but has been lingering in the background of our thoughts. Life is like a race and it is very important to focus on staying in your lane and looking straight ahead at your objective.

The thorniest issue by far is when you take an astronomical leap into a higher financial status. Simply put, your success may just make some folks uncomfortable. This is when the rubber hits the road—when the blindfold of cultural context is finally lifted from your friends' eyes. Here is when they see that yes! Those wild ideas you always talked of indeed had merit. Yes! A person with the same blueprint as mine can change his entire lifestyle by confronting and changing his cultural context. "Now HOW did you say you did that?" many will ask.

Change in you may bring about change in others.

You may have to choose between your friends being uncomfortable, or being comfortable in your own skin.

Role Models—A Careful Selection

Role models are like old wives' tales: you believe them until experience teaches you different. Role models are different than friends and parents because they teach us without our having to barter for acceptance.

One of my most significant role models was my stepfather, Andrew, a man I loved and respected. He taught me an important lesson—that when it comes to cultural context, we have options. We can choose exactly what we will do with the blueprint we've received: accept, modify, reject, or get a new one.

Andrew worked just about everyday at a local factory. His monthly ritual was to pay bills painstakingly while reminiscing that he'd attended college for two years. Factory work was safe, he said—it paid the bills and fed six children. I assumed that because I was younger, Andrew was right and I was wrong. However, I could never quite grasp his logic. I never got up the nerve to ask him, "When did you stop trying?"

Prior to Andrew, my role model was a guy married to a witch. While many of my friends were mimicking James Bond—free falling out of pretend airplanes and wiggling out of impossible predicaments, I was giving high-fives to Darren Stevens of *Bewitched*. Darren had only one nemesis in life: a mother-in-law named Endora who couldn't get "Derwood's" name right if her life depended on it. The show's continuous plot revolved around him getting Endora and other precipitous characters out of his life and back to Witchville, where they belonged.

In my eyes, Darren was one smooth guy who had it all—a beautiful wife who could outwit his enemies at the twitch of her nose, designer suits that fit flawlessly, and a job that brought him home in time for dinner most nights. Darren's life was just as exciting as James Bond's, and he never sweated over paying bills.

Then I was exposed to a different model, an event which drastically altered the course of my life. As a salesman at J.C. Penney, I scraped for customers and competed against coworkers for commissions that seldom exceeded $300 a week. This job gave my parents unabashed bragging rights—I was making what they called "good money," and I purchased a new car, a Pontiac Grand Prix. In their eyes, I had "arrived." In most instances, this meant I would forego college and have to work and pay bills for the term of the car loan. Thank God things worked out a bit differently, but we'll get back to that later.

One day at J.C Penney, in walked a guy selling roller skates to the store. His take for one hour of work? $3,000—10 times my pay for an entire back-breaking week! At that moment, I knew there was a better way—I could make money I had never dreamed of by selling *to* a retailer rather than *for* a retailer.

Meanwhile, my cultural context said I had hit pay dirt with that $300-a-week job. I was at a critical point in my life, faced with two choices: embrace my stepfather's approach and accept that $300 as "good money," or wipe the slate clean and redefine myself based on a different model. I was to learn one of the most important lessons in my life—don't cast yourself too soon and reject positive experiences because of the constant reinforcement of your cultural context.

Solutions To Dealing With Cultural Context—First You Must Examine

A healthy person habitually examines their baggage to review what's still working and what no longer works. As with the first sentence in a novel, we start at the beginning. We do this by gaining an understanding of our cultural contexts and the places they have in our lives. Knowing their placement enables us to choose their prominence. This is like performing surgery as we cut away the membranes of dead weight. Remember why it's called baggage—it's something that you carry with you.

Your dreams may come to you in the middle of the night, but plowing through a lifetime of cultural context is no overnight task. If your dream is to become an astronaut and you refuse to entertain that desire due to your cultural context, then that's not a good thing. Why? Because when you wake up in the morning, you still want to be that astronaut.

Evaluating your cultural context initiates the process of changing your most powerful asset: your mind. You then are faced with a choice—you can take the path of least resistance, or realize that you may be in for the fight of your life. Resist the temptation to settle for mediocrity rather than striving for the best.

If you find that your current cultural context conflicts with a set of more positive experiences, such as making $3,000 versus $300 per week, or being an astronaut instead of an assembly line worker, then adopt that new baggage.

Be Wary of the Assumptions You Make

My stepfather, Andrew, reinforced the idea that factory work was *the* best option for a career. My parents' expression that I was making "good money" at Penney's reinforced the idea that college was not for me. I didn't understand at the time that "good money" is a phrase people use to describe earning a significant amount within the bounds of their exposure. To them, I was well within the range of my expected earning potential.

This was further enhanced during high school—not one counselor asked if I intended to attend college.

Before meeting the roller skate guy, I assumed that working at a factory or at Penney's were reasonable careers and the only options available to me. I didn't understand that the cultural context handed down to me included a set of established guidelines. The most critical assumption was that I had no options other than those that fell within rigid guidelines. The others were that I was not supposed to attend college and that $300 per week was the answer to not sweating over bills.

Assumptions can be misleading—they represent dismissal prior to investigation, when the answer is an open mind.

Practice Humility

Family, friends, and people we admire—how would we survive without them? We don't. The answer is humility—acceptance of their views without rejection of our own. We recognize that our parents and friends played a key role in getting us where we are today, and that they will always have our backs, no matter how far up the ladder we may climb. We modify the cultural baggage but keep the love.

Stay Balanced

Keep in mind that wealth is not the primary objective of examining our cultural contexts. More importantly than that, it is our belief that we are fulfilling the purposes for our lives. Some people have cultural contexts that work totally in conflict with their life objectives. They may operate based upon short-term financial objectives. They may buy into an unhealthy corporate machine. To value their stake holders, this group of people should shed this baggage and live lives based on their visions. In such cases, we learn to embrace humanity, even if we keep the view that profits, love, and humanity are compatible.

Revise Your Starting Point

Living outside prescribed guidelines presents a double-edged sword—you can be ostracized for failing to live within them, and for exceeding them. For example, if you are in the middle-income bracket, your guiding principle dictates that you remain middle income. If you fail to achieve middle class status, you are seen as a failure. However, when you exceed middle class, you lose its built-in support system. You relinquish it because your cultural context is set up for you to achieve a level similar to the people who surround you.

If you soar way beyond the established guideposts, you will at some point become counter-cultural. Counter-culture happens when you go against your environment, changing the trajectory or possibilities for your life. Let's say your father and siblings make $25,000 annually. Your father owns a corner store, and when he retires, you're expected to take it over. Your earning expectation is $25,000. But if you decide to attend college, your trajectory could change to $50,000—you've just changed your expectations and can now map the trajectory of your children's lives starting at $50,000.

Continuously Review Your Core Beliefs

The vision Ford introduced over 100 years ago was based on the now defunct X management style (versus theory Y). This form of management relied heavily on microscopic control of employees to achieve high productivity at low cost. But micromanagement was merely a sign of those times—from the workplace to raising children—and there was little tolerance for freedom of thought. Supervisors told employees what to do and parents told their children what to do. This style of management met its demise through introduction of a global economy and the Internet. The new venue of "knowledge is power" ushered in an appreciation for creativity, problem solving, and teamwork. Change should be embraced, not feared.

Get Ready for the Journey of Your Life

Start packing—you're going on a new journey. You've scrutinized your baggage, kept some, and tossed some. Now the challenge is to make peace with your *own* ghosts. That's because the biggest battle doesn't come from without, it comes from within. This is an inside job in which you take full responsibility for matching your intuition with your outer actions.

To set up new guidelines based on your own purpose, you will need to embrace new experiences and options. Dreaming of becoming an astronaut? Surround yourself with astronauts. Visit science fairs. Join associations and support groups. Desire to be a top-notch fashion designer? Hit the runways and galas in New York and Paris so you can learn from the best. Identify with the best of whatever it is you want to do and adopt their positive attributes (yes, we're still using best practices). Remember, imitation is the best form of flattery, but some day, someone may be imitating *you*.

Finally, We Must Reconcile

To enjoy life to its fullest by YOUR definition, you've got to reconcile those opposing voices with what's in YOUR heart. This is an inside job—you need inner strength to cut through inner voices. Resolutely ask yourself: *Are my decisions and I good bedfellows? How well do we sleep together at night? Do I retain unhealthy beliefs at the expense of my peace of mind? Am I willing to let go of my security blanket of acceptance from those who may lack understanding of a path only I can see? Can I cast off the self-doubt imposed by others, and at times, myself?*

We all have a still, small voice that communicates answers quite loudly. It is absolutely up to us to understand, trust, and act upon that small voice. A common definition for faith is "belief in things unseen". It is now up to you to exercise faith in the vision that the small voice whispers in your ear.

Exercises

1. You are a unique creation. Khalil Gibran described our children as arrows sent forth into life from their parents' bow. It is the parents' job is to provide guidance for the child's flight. You are a new creation with a journey of your own. Your life experiences have much the same effect, providing similar guidance. They shape you and help you understand which mistakes you should not repeat. No matter where you are from or the circumstances of your life, you have a unique purpose that you must begin to carry out. You must use all of your experiences, good and bad, to shape your vision for your life. Do the following:

   > Close your eyes and listen to the small voice within you that knows why you were created, and write down your vision. For some, the first inner voice they hear is the critical voice, like fear, acknowledge that critical voice, learn from it. Now, search for that positive inner voice that has been longing for your attention for so long. Let your creative inner voice lead you to wonderful, prosperous, and powerful new things.

> Your cultural context is the voice that attempts to put a limit on your vision. It attempts to tie you to your past. Think about the influences in your life that are in conflict with this vision. Write each of them down on a piece of paper. Strike the ones that do not apply to you. I'll bet that none of them apply to your current circumstance.

> Decide which influences should be part of your life and which should not. This is where you determine if your vision has value to you.

2. Except for situations of abuse, it is not healthy to make a tremendous number of changes in your life without much contemplation. Please understand that you were created for greatness in whatever you do. Never settle for less.

NOTE:

Arkansas is one of the poorest states in the country. I am sure that Bill Clinton had many opportunities to ignore the vision for his life. I am also sure he ignored all of the negative voices on his way to becoming the President of the United States of America. How are you handling your voices from inside and outside?

A Little Story

The Green Bay Packers never lost a football game. They just ran out of time.

—Vince Lombardi

Vince Lombardi was one of the most successful coaches in American football history. Known for inspiring and motivating his players, he led the Green Bay Packers to five National Football League (NFL) championships, as well as victories in the first two Super Bowls.

Before Lombardi became their coach, the Packers hadn't had a winning season in a decade. They had finished last in their conference the previous two years, winning just three of twelve games in 1957. In 1958, they won one game.

One game? They won—not lost—ONE GAME?

Then, along came Lombardi. The Packers won seven games in his first year as coach. The following year, they lost only one *crucial* game—the 1960 NFL championship—to the Philadelphia Eagles. The next year, they captured their first NFL title under Lombardi, trouncing the Giants 37-0 in the championship game. What do you think the Packers' culture was like before Lombardi? Let's do the math. They were LOSING. Well-meaning fans knew deep in their hearts that the Packers were going to lose. Even other losing teams expected to beat the Packers! Those partners in defeat may have barely won three games themselves, but bless their hearts, they KNEW at least one victory would be against those Packers!

Fast forward to the mid-sixties. The Packers were

in their hey-day, the hottest team on the planet. If you never stepped a toe out on that field but were a Green Bay Packer, you were STILL a winner. Vince Lombardi had introduced a new culture. The Packers had dumped their old culture of losing and were now regaling in the thrill of victory!

CHAPTER 4
THE BASICS OF YOUR LIFE PLAN

If you don't know where you are going, you will wind up somewhere else.

—Yogi Berra

Your wife smiles. Reminiscing, she muses about a secret the two of you shared: your daily greeting that consisted of a simple, light touch on the small of her back.

Laughter erupts among the crowd. Your daughter is recalling that you *always* bumped your head when entering the attic—so much that it became a family joke.

The growing pains of becoming a young man didn't seem so rough, your son notes—not with a Dad who never said, "I told you so" when you made a mistake.

Silently, each family member remembers you in their own special way. It's been a good life. Even your mother-in-law, who swore you were NOT the one for her daughter, looks on you with respect.

Imagine that today is your funeral. This is the last time the most important people in your life will lay eyes on you. At the final moment, will these be the thoughts running through their minds? Or will there be regret? Regret that most days, your only welcome was a plate of food gone cold hours ago because you worked until nine p.m. Regret that you never understood that your daily head-bumping ritual made you seem 10 feet tall in your daughter's eyes. Regret that your son ponders his position as a man in this world because you never took the time to validate him.

Granted, these cases may appear a bit extreme. What's *not* extreme, however, is that at some point, you will face the ending stage of your life. The important thought to ponder is, given the chance to look back over your life, what would *you* think? Would you make different decisions if only you had the time? Or the money?

Up to this point, we've confronted the juggernaut of mindless spending and defeatist thinking. But you can spend wisely and think positively with great success, and unless accompanied by action, the results will be nil. Before you act, however, you need to have a plan.

This chapter is about the importance of developing a plan for your life. The objective is to prepare you to create a carefully considered plan that enables you to connect sound economic decisions to your goals.

What Is a Life Plan?

A life plan is your blueprint for your life. It outlines what you want to accomplish, how you plan to go about it, and when. If you get off track, your life plan will serve as a guidepost for keeping you focused.

So, what does wishing for more time have to do with a life plan? It is crucial to understand *as soon as possible* where you want to go so you can spend the *majority* of your time getting there. Tailoring your life plan with your funeral in mind focuses your attention and energy on goals and activities that you wish or need to accomplish. You are then less apt to end up someplace you don't want to be, dragging your loved ones right along with you.

Why Is a Life Plan So Important?

For many of us, developing a life plan is our first concerted effort to change the courses of our lives. This plan is important because it combats inertia—it revs our imagination, gets our juices rolling, forces us to deliberate our purpose in life. It begs the question, "Do I want my life to unfold accidentally or with purpose?" We likely will find that the degree to which we plan is directly proportional to our degree of control.

Someone once said, "The best way to predict the future is to create it."

A major benefit of a life plan is that it puts you in the driver's seat in deciding your socioeconomic status. To see how this works, let's say you map out a life plan and decide you want to be a dentist. This makes you a doctor. Doctors are expected to look professional, conduct themselves in a professional manner, keep their own bodies healthy, not smoke or drink excessively—you get the picture. But doctors generally are respected—politicians, government agencies, and clergy seek out their opinions on a myriad of issues. This automatically places them in the category of civic leaders.

Here's the catch—people in higher economic circles are what I call "perk-privy." When you become a dentist, a doctor, or an executive, you enter a world where you are privileged to perks not easily accessible to average citizens. This is not because those in different economic circles don't know about them or cannot somehow obtain them. It's because they usually lack the status and money to afford them.

This example in no way implies that you must obtain any socioeconomic status to be happy. In fact, along my life journey, I can say that status or money had nothing to do with happiness at any point. In fact, I can honestly say that perceived socioeconomic status and perceived wealth has gotten in the way of what might have otherwise been good, healthy relationships. I can also say that the accumulation of wealth will highlight your flaws. The point is that everyone has a purpose in life. Once you understand and become comfortable with how you are to contribute to the world—*your purpose*—you are ready to put a plan in place. Happiness is achieved through maintaining a proper balance between what is important in your life apart from your pursuit of that purpose. Money and the accumulation of wealth have their place in this pursuit, but it is absolutely not the focus or the reward.

Your Stakeholders—The Most Important Reason for Developing a Life Plan

In Chapter 1, I briefly noted that each household is its own economy, with expenses, income, taxes, and so on. Corporations have the same basic financial structure, except they are much more complex. But unlike many households, corporations pay close attention to financial targets or objectives. The primary reason for such focus is that all enterprises have stakeholders. They are the people who purchase stock in companies, i.e., provide capital for its existence. If the corporation is not meeting its target objectives, then the stakeholders become unhappy and take their money away. No money, no corporation. All successful corporations know that their most important job is to make sure their stakeholders are pleased.

Before you put pen to paper, you should get a clear understanding of who your stakeholders are. Ask yourself, *Who matters most to me?* I would argue that in a family enterprise, your children, spouse, and anyone who depends on you are your stakeholders. Knowing who your stakeholders are is an important aspect of your life plan because you will always know what matters most. You will also be keenly aware of how your financial decisions impact those who matter most.

The Connection Between Economic Decisions and Your Life Plan

Economic decisions should be one of the highest priorities in your life plan for two reasons. The first reason is that if you don't seriously consider each economic decision, you take a chance on making a range of ill-fated choices. The impact of a financial life without consideration can range from low-level discontent to downright disaster. You could be frustrated in the long run, which ultimately could shorten your life. The second reason is that while money may never change you, it absolutely changes your environment and your socioeconomic position—both of which affect the quality of your life.

When aligned with sound economic decisions, your life plan positions you to take the guesswork out of life and eliminate as many "what ifs" as possible.

You can then focus on achieving your desired outcome—at least the parts over which you have control.

Time Is Money

A life plan and economic decisions share one common
denominator—both impact every area of your life. The
connection between the two lies in a simple concept. It
is a financial axiom that if you struggle with money,
you will struggle with time. When you make bad economic decisions, it takes time to correct them. If your
economic decisions are not aligned appropriately, it
may take you two to three times as long to understand
where you want to go or should go.

No matter what your age, bad decisions can be a
bitter pill to swallow, especially if they result in financial struggles. When this occurs, you are not enjoying
life; you're either running from it or trying to catch up
with it. And this is not the worst of it—when you finally determine where you're supposed to go, it will take
you even more years to get there.

Our main job in living our lives is to make decisions
and act on them. Unfortunately, we often do not have
the tools to make good ones. We must always remember that good decisions are made consistently with our
objectives. Our life plans help to establish our objectives. This process keeps us heading in the straightest
line possible, eliminating the accidental and many times
painful detours that consume years of our time. I will
walk you through building a life plan in the next chapter. Before doing so, I will share a few points to remember and explain the basic components of the plan.

Your Future and Your Plan Are One and the Same

Let's explore the concept of developing a life plan using a simple exercise. Instead of waiting to look *back* over your life, start at this moment thinking of your life in future terms. Try to focus on what you *would* accomplish in your life if someone handed it to you on a silver platter. The good news is that you're NOT at the end of your life, which means you have the opportunity to make sound decisions while they are in your grasp.

Get Answers to Two Questions Before Starting Your Plan

In order to develop a life plan, you first must figure out two things: what you DON'T want to do and how much money you want to make. Knowing what you don't want to do prevents you from investing time and energy on activities that can sidetrack or prevent you from achieving your goals in life. If you know that you are doing something that you don't want to do for the rest of your life and know the area that you want to pursue, that is a start. Now, let's get you going in the right direction. Knowing how much money you want to make will help you align your economic decisions with your goals. I will demonstrate how to get these answers as I walk through the plan in the next chapter. I will also show you how I used these tactics to achieve my objectives.

Use Your Personal Life Plan as Your Bible

The magnitude of careful thought cannot be understated when it comes to developing your life plan. A life plan must be dynamic. You must be willing to evaluate your progress against your objectives, and if they change based on your life circumstances, have the courage to adjust your plan to achieve the quality of life you desire.

If you belong to a religious body or practice some form of spirituality, draw on your beliefs as you approach this endeavor. Ask for wisdom, strength and direction. Remember, your personal life plan is your way of protecting your current stakeholders and the loved ones of your future.

Seek Quality Over Quantity

We live in a $56 TRILLION global economy, so you'll want to make decisions that greatly enhance your chances of getting a nice chunk of it. The size of that chunk, however, should be based on what gives you and your stakeholders the peace of mind to enjoy it.

Economic freedom is an important aspect of a high-quality life, but it is only a sidebar to true contentment. I do not purport to define nor decide what makes each individual happy. If making tons of money is your main focus, that's just grand. If making tons of money is your ONLY focus, that's not so great.. The premise of the life plan is to build a whole and balanced life, which cannot easily be achieved if you're struggling financially and find yourself more concerned with economic issues than with those you love.

Exercises:

1. Write your eulogy.

2. Describe the people that are attending your funeral. If you do not have people that are close to you today, create them. Who would you like to be in your future? This is your time to dream.

3. Write down what each person says about you. What would you like them to say?

4. Name your stakeholders if possible.

CHAPTER 5
FINDING YOUR YELLOW BRICK ROAD

You have a unique vision for your life. Let's find it, trust it, and make decisions to support it.

A life plan consists of the following basic components: vision, mission statement, core values, and objectives. I will explore each of these as we walk through development of a life plan.

It All Starts With a Vision

Your plan always begins with your vision, not from where you are right now. A vision says, "I'm not there yet, but at least I know where I'm going." Crafting a plan as if you're at the end of your life allows you to create the life you want to live. This vision should answer specific questions. What do I want to see at the end of my life? What would make me proud? How will my loved ones feel? Keep in mind the principle, "In order to be it, you first have to see it." Is there something inside of you that keeps you up at night? When you want to think about something else, that same thought creeps back into your mind. Or does your vision speak to you quietly, with consistency? Either way, if you are clear about the calling of your life, that is your vision. Do you want to be a housewife, a computer programmer, or a dancer? For me, the path to my vision unfolded at different "ah-ha" moments. Some that I could not ignore felt like this:

> Visiting a meat packing plant in high school and seeing a man with a finger missing still cutting meat with the same saw. I knew from that point forward I DID NOT want to work around dangerous equipment.

> The high school counselor suggesting that I learn a trade, such as carpentry. This just did not make sense to me or feel quite right when I saw many of my classmates discussing different colleges.

> I knew that I did not like working in retail, and felt that I was more capable than my boss, who had a college degree. This clearly meant that I needed to obtain one, but in what field?

> While working in retail, coming to terms with the fact that I loved selling and helping people.

> Meeting a roller skate salesman who probably made 10 times the money I made because he had a degree and could sell skates. Again, I knew that I needed a college degree.

> My friend told me that he enlisted in the Air Force to help him finish his college degree. I joined him.

> Working for a computer manufacturer as a programmer, I met a salesman and decided I could and would do that job. I spent the next 10 years pursuing work in computer sales. I realized that my degree should be in computer science and marketing.

> While working on the same job as a systems analyst for the next six years and finishing my degree, I knew that my next step was to get promoted into computer sales.

> Being told that if I wanted to be in business I should be

in business all the way and discontinue my relationship with my current employer. This was scary to be forced to operate a business with no type of a safety net. This moment propelled me into my company Scientific & Engineering Solutions.

The events mentioned here helped me figure out what I did not want to do in my life professionally. By default, I began to understand more about what I wanted to do. If something did not feel right, I changed what I was doing and moved toward whatever made more sense for me and my life. You should not expect to get a mysteriously written tablet that just shows up and gives you directions. Look for direction and guideposts in your life. You must observe them and continue to move forward. You must not be afraid to make changes. To be stagnant and discontent can be a miserable experience for both you and your loved ones.

The Mission Statement—What Is My Purpose?

Once you have crystallized your vision, you will need to establish a mission statement. A mission statement bottom-lines your purpose for being here. It states the axiom of your existence and answers the question, "Why was I put on this earth?"

Your Core Values

Face it—life simply doesn't always go our way. Couple this reality with trials, tests, temptations, or even discouragement at times, and you've placed yourself smack in the middle of what is called LIFE. With life being what it is, riddled with ups, downs, and surprises, you have to stand for something or fall for anything.

Values are your concrete beliefs or set of principles that remain the same in spite of change. They are your compass and conscience, quietly governing how you operate in life and relate to your family, friends, and community. Values state what you believe and what's important to you. Is it important that your children get a good night's sleep so they can do well in school? How do you even know if they are home, let alone sleeping, if you get home from work at 10:30 every night? Are you valuing your job or your child's education? Is your son's self-esteem of value to you? If so, then what the heck are you doing at the office while he's playing his first basketball game?

If your quest to achieve your vision opposes what you believe in, you may want to rethink that vision; to do otherwise would attach conflict to your dreams. And if you've worked hard to eliminate baggage from your life, then you realize that the heaviest luggage usually lies within you.

As you strive for your vision, use your value system to keep you centered, emotionally healthy, and guilt-free.

Objectives

Objectives are the meat and potatoes of a life plan. They help you determine all of the activities you need to perform in order to achieve your goal. Without them, you will potentially live a life that takes you and your family in circles, and you likely will waste a lot of time.

Objectives should be viewed in terms of short-term

goals (milestones), mid-term goals, and long-term goals (strategic objectives), all of which must always have specific timeframes attached to them. For example, they should answer the question, "Where do I see myself in 1, 5, and 10 years?"

With a clear view of where you want to go, you can use objectives to map out a plan consisting of specific actions that will help you achieve the milestones. The important thing to remember is that once you clearly visualize what your life will be like in the timeframe you have established, you should at that moment start working toward those objectives.

Your Life Plan—The Road to Freedom

I would argue that one of the worst occurrences is having a life full of regrets as you approach the end of it. This is particularly painful if you know you could have done things differently but chose not to—not because you didn't desire to, but because you simply didn't give your life enough thought. This activity should help you to look at yourself honestly. It should help you understand your role in the events that occur in your life. You are the architect of your life. You set the climate, the tone, the direction, and you even make choices about how you will feel from day to day. You decide how you will respond to life events.

I believe the best way to think of a life plan and your life's objectives is to picture the map in a mall, with the red letters and arrow stating, "YOU ARE HERE!" This is the starting point for your life plan; this represents today. Now, continue to picture this map and overlay it with your life and the destination you would like to reach. What choices will you have to make to get there? What will you do when you get to those intersections that you cannot anticipate, such as when you must care for an aging parent, or face a family illness or disability? You can plan to navigate through many different circumstances to achieve your objectives. Your personal life plan is the first and ongoing step to this freedom.

Exercises:

1. Write your life's vision.

2. Write your 'ah ha' moments.

3. Write your life's mission.

4. Write a series of objectives that help you to accomplish your vision and mission. Remember to focus on what is important!

CHAPTER 6
DEVELOPING YOUR LIFE PLAN

You are the author of your own life story.
—Sign in the sixth grade classroom of
Ascension Lutheran School,
Landover Hills, Maryland

It's time to create your life plan. My hope is that you will gain a glimpse of how economic decisions play a vital role in living the life you choose. If you have a spouse or significant other, it is recommended that you involve them in this process.

Create Your Vision

Your vision begins with your imagination. Instead of visualizing your funeral, fantasize. This exercise works best when you close your eyes, so after you read the next few sentences, close your eyes, bask in the vision, and then write down what you saw with your mind's eye.

What type of car are you driving? Is it blue or green? Is it a convertible that allows your hair to blow in the wind? When you pull into your driveway every day, what's the vision of your home? Is it a brownstone or a colonial? Does it have a white picket fence? What color is it? Are the grounds neatly manicured, resembling an image from *Better Homes and Gardens*? Who greets you when you arrive home? Two kids who look forward to playing Scrabble with you because you think you're *so* smart? A wife, husband, or significant other waiting for that special touch? What's cooking on the grill? Is the aroma of sizzling steak and salmon inviting you to dine? What are your neighbors like? Are they doctors, lawyers, executives, trades people or business owners? What public schools are near your home? Are they top-notch, with a waiting list from kids outside the school district vying for a spot?

When you have finished visualizing your lifestyle, start calculating the price of your vision.

Answer the First of Two Crucial Questions— The Price of Your Vision

Perhaps you envisioned a brownstone home in a ritzy district with schools that prepare your kids for the nation's top colleges. This home costs $400,000. With interest rates at seven percent on a 30-year mortgage, you're roughly looking at a $2,661 monthly house note. Your Mercedes convertible with all the trimmings costs $60,000. A $5,000 down payment might put your monthly car note at $800. Add utilities, food, recreation, vacations, and possibly day care, and you require about $6,000 monthly to experience your vision.

Does the price of this vision match what you want to do professionally? If not, you have to be willing to make adjustments to your occupation or your vision. If not, your life could be one of frustration.

Incorporate Your Values

The cost of day care would likely mean you and your spouse work outside the home. This would be fine, except you and your spouse—a stakeholder—agreed that one of you would raise the kids at home until they were school age. You envisioned your children attending a reputable neighborhood school so they would be home in time to greet you, too.

When establishing your values, you decided that your stakeholders were a driving force for your vision. To achieve cohesion between your values, loved ones, and vision, you would need to become a single wage earner. So, you would now need to earn over $8,000 a month, or $100,000 annually.

Determine Your Objectives

Exactly what do you need to do to earn $100,000 in, say, five years? Objectives clarify this. It is almost impossible to yield tangible results without attaching specific objectives and timeframes to your life plan.

As discussed in the previous chapter, companies thrive on meeting objectives because they measure progress and success. For example, corporations focus on meeting targeted earnings per share—the amount of profit gained by each share of stock. Earnings per share are usually behind the firing of many top chief executive officers. A CEO can recreate an organization's culture, motivate retirees to come back, and even reinvent a few wheels. But if they don't meet their earnings per share target, the board of directors will find someone else to head the organization. The same concept applies to people who work in sales. If a salesperson fails to hit their objectives, they won't have that job very long. Staying focused on your objectives lets you gauge the pulse of your entire efforts—whether you are on the mark, falling behind, or on the wrong track. As a family member and as an employee, you should have your own income targets or objectives, just as corporations do, and take those objectives seriously, as they do. Cement this goal in your head by writing it down and use each year as a milestone to gauge your progress.

Objectives are therefore a critical mechanism for taking control of your life and achieving what you determine to be reasonable. They help you monitor your progress to determine if or when you get off track. If you happen to get off track, you can then make decisions that put you back in place. The most important aspect of setting objectives is that even if you reach 80 percent of them, you are so much farther ahead than if you had set no objectives at all.

Slice Your Objectives Into Manageable Tasks

Let's say you are 25 years old, making $40,000 a year. Your overall goal is to earn $100,000 by the time you're 30. Calculate the difference between $40,000 and $100,000 over five years—the difference is $60,000, meaning you would need to escalate your income more than $12,000 a year. You've just narrowed your objective into a more concrete goal.

No matter what your current financial status, your five-year objective remains the same: to close that $60,000 gap. Seems like a tall order, doesn't it? Darn right. What's at stake, however, is the vision you've established for your loved ones. Remember, your vision is based in future terms, not where you are now, so it is redundant to think in terms of what *cannot* be done. This is too valuable to change, dilute, or eliminate simply because it looks tough. But it's not impossible. Your job, then, is to sort out what you're going to do. In business terms, this is known as "strategic thinking."

Simply put, strategic thinking aligns your mission statement or purpose with your financial goals. Here, you relate back to the question, "What is my reason for being here and why is this so important?" And since it is unlikely that $60,000 is growing in your economic garden, you've got to look to your external environment (such as the American economy, the work world, and so on) to obtain it. Fortunately, America's economic minefield is a lot richer than mine—to the tune of $17 trillion. What is my creative response or strategy to obtaining some of this $17 trillion?

A good starting point is to narrow your employment considerations to jobs most likely to pay you $100,000 in five years. The second step is to set up income objectives that you will hit annually. An effective approach to this is employing best practices. These are some of your new tactical objectives or milestones.

Apply Best Practices to Your Vision

Many people approach paying bills as a dismal chore—too many bills, not enough money. And some people do this month after month, *ad infinitum*! But you're reading this book because you've decided to get out of the problem and into a solution.

You've set your sights on a mid-term goal, not a monthly trauma. One proven formula for conquering what appears to be an insurmountable objective—like increasing your income $60,000 in five years—is to associate yourself with people who have already accomplished this feat. Ask and watch how they reached their goals, then apply their methods to your life on a regular basis. If the person or people you choose do not willingly share, ask others. You must not be denied!

The Importance of Association, Education, and Development in Achieving Your Vision— Iron Sharpens Iron

If you hang around a hot dog stand, eventually you will buy one. Similarly, one of the most important strategies for achieving success is to associate with successful people. You are more than likely very comfortable with your daily experiences and can navigate your current circumstances with some ease. In order to achieve the objectives that you will put in place, however, you must step out of that comfort zone. Step into unfamiliar territory, and remember it is a part of the vision that you have for your life.

Seek out organizations that specialize in the area of

your vision—trade publications, associations, or any other source that can help you focus your plan on effective measures. Asking for help is also a good exercise in humility—it reminds you to remain teachable for the remainder of your life and to help others once you achieve a measure of success.

Stick With the Rules—Educate Yourself

Another form of best practices is higher education. As stated in Chapter 1, the global financial infrastructure in most cases supports higher education by rewarding those who have advanced degrees with higher-paying jobs. This automatically makes higher education a best practice. By contrast, those who lack it often find their salaries coming to a screeching halt, particularly as they reach the later stages of life.

According to the *New Economy Index*, a Web publication that provides economic analysis, a key factor in the increasing earnings gap has been the increased wage premium paid to higher education and skills. Since the 1970s, the article states, college graduates' salaries have continued to rise, while those with less than a bachelor's degree, particularly those with a high school degree or less, have seen their real wages fall.

How many of you know a college dropout who was lured by quick money? The average student just doesn't have lots of money to throw around; in fact, most are downright broke. Earning $20 an hour at Sam's Butcher Shop can be mighty tempting if your staple foods have been peanut butter and jelly sandwiches and canned tuna for the last two years. The economic consideration is, what is the likelihood of this job turning into $100,000 within five years? If the senior butcher is pulling in $25,000 annually and bragging about it, you *know* you can kiss that $100,000 vision goodbye! The surest way to get locked into a salary is not to have an education. Deciding to acquire a degree is an economic decision because it is a long-term investment that you expect to yield high returns. Another way to put this is, in order to get money, you have to spend money. College degrees position you for upward mobility. You also gain flexibility to change jobs or even careers if you want to make huge financial strides.

Your next objective is to achieve the education level required to get a job that could potentially pay $100,000 a year. Due to the changing economic landscape, an associates degree can add a good amount of value. Consider all of your options.

Think Long-Term Investment in Yourself

To see how this works, let's say you work either in the field of human resources or medicine. It is not unusual for executives such as vice presidents of human resources (VP of HR) to earn $100,000 annually. Dentists, doctors, entrepreneurs, and salespeople can earn twice this amount and more.

First, closely analyze the education required to become VP of HR or a dentist. If you view the qualifications for becoming the VP of HR, more than likely the minimum education requirement would be a bachelor's degree, and perhaps a graduate degree. The total time investment would be four years to obtain the bachelor's and three years to earn the graduate degree, for a total investment of seven years. Looking closer, it would take about the same amount of time to become a dentist—four years of undergraduate work and four years of dental school. The point here is, when embarking on your career, start with the financial outcome in mind, and then align your decisions with the outcome.

Development and Opportunity Equal Success

Ever meet a smart person who succeeded in the classroom but couldn't seem to get ahead professionally? Or the person who could do the job well on paper but couldn't get along with anyone? You're going to need more than an education to achieve your objectives.

Executive level employees are usually selected, trained, and groomed. Once you achieve a high socioeconomic level, you want to *stay* there. To do this, you first need to establish objectives that provide you with the technical skills so you will at least be considered for higher-level jobs. You then will need to develop continuously the finesse and communications skills to navigate smoothly the world of those already there.

For example, let's say you're a 50-year-old computer programmer and want to revamp your career. It's a great job and pays well, but a $15,000 annual raise isn't likely. You've been thinking of moving up to another level but have become stagnated because technology is synonymous with change. To change means you would have to adapt to the new lightning-speed era of technological innovation. To reach a higher level, you would need to get training in areas unheard of when you were getting a computer science degree 30 years ago, such as Web applications, wireless technology, and so on.

But successful executives must possess more than technological skills. If the gift of gab is not one of your strengths, you may have to build into your plan some training that will give you the confidence to present yourself effectively to the person who gives raises. If you have the boss's ear, you may have only one shot to get it right.

I am what you would probably call a classic introvert. I used to watch people engage in small talk and wonder, *How do they just stand there and talk about nothing?* I had a boss who was really good at forming relationships by engaging people in small talk. I really can't remember when it happened, but after practice and more practice, I found myself engaged in small talk with potential customers. I did use a strategy, however. I would look around the office of the executive I was visiting and pick out an item I found interesting and knew something about. I then asked the customer an educated question about something that was probably important to him or her. This worked well—after about 15 minutes of chatting, business matters came much easier, and it was good to learn about the person.

Know Your Stuff, and More Importantly, Your Organization

Your immediate objective is to get noticed in your current organization. You've gone back to school and obtained a master's degree, but with the slew of online degrees available to the masses, you're finding it difficult to distinguish yourself. Frankly, no one has these expectations for your life except you. One of your first objectives here is to make sure you are in a company that values your efforts.

Many executives are not experts in the nitty-gritty operations of an organization, but they are well versed in their organization's core purpose. One of the best ways to get positive attention is to know as much as possible about your organization. A good way to achieve this is to go above and beyond the call of duty. If your work hours are eight to five, you would get noticed by coming in at 7:30 and leaving at 5:30, and using that time to learn all you can about the organization.

Because you have been developing yourself personally and professionally, you are no longer on the sidelines, wishing for a position that will change your socioeconomic status. You're in the running because your development travels have taught you the one phrase that is music to all GOOD companies' ears: "I want to bring value to our organization."

Never Underestimate the Power of Politics

The above statement meets the objective of being seen in a positive light by those who have the power to select you for a different position. To achieve this, you must become aware of the kind of communication decision makers in organizations love to hear, and more importantly, mean what you're saying.

For example, let's say the CEO comes in early and stays late, too. You now have the opportunity to chat with him or her on a more informal basis. One day, the CEO inquires how you like the company and how you see your career path. You've groomed yourself for this opportunity and this is your time to shine! Your points-winning response would be, "I want to make sure that my work brings value to the corporation. I want to make sure that I achieve my personal life plan, and I will work as hard as it takes to make sure that this company is successful and that I share in that success."

In so doing, be sure to inform your superior, with all honesty, that salary is secondary to incentives as compensation, because it is the executive position that will provide you access to upward mobility and access to all the perks. In no case should you embrace motives or actions that make your superior feel that your motivation is just to make more money—doing so could make you appear greedy and insincere about wanting to help the company.

At the appropriate time, such as prior to the beginning of the calendar or fiscal year, or whatever cycle your company supports, you should make your plans for moving up in the organization known to your manager. Ask for guidance and direction as to how to accomplish your objective. The most effective method for this discussion is first to pick a career path that will bring value to the organization and get buy-in from management. Simply put, figure out what's important to your manager and make sure that she is clear that you want to help achieve her objective.

At this point, you should both agree that this additional work will have a positive impact on the company and your career. Again, the focus at this point is not on money, but rather on visibility within the organization and ability to make large strides. Remember, your objective is to get a $60,000 increase in five years, which would require you to earn several promotions. To achieve such a jump, management would have to view you as a leader in that organization.

Learn to Pick Your Battles— The Stakeholder Must Always Win

Flexibility is a key component to keeping emotional balance while pursuing your vision. What if this economic decision to earn $100,000 annually by being a VP of HR doesn't quite match your personality? It bugs you to no end when your boss asks you to stay two hours late to prepare for an executive briefing. You are hungry and you want to go HOME! It's time for an attitude adjustment. Before jumping ship, weigh the job requirements against a bigger playing field and your preset values. Working two hours late once a week may be worth the sacrifice if your general lifestyle entails getting home at a reasonable hour and spending most evenings with your children and spouse—making $100,000 a year.

All of your decisions should be adaptable, clear to your loved ones, and aligned with your values. For example, the culture of lawyers is to work a lot of hours. If legal work is your passion, and you and your stakeholders have agreed that working in a profession you love is a high priority, then long hours are not a negative aspect of your life plan. On the other hand, if your value system embraces being free in the evenings, then a job in the medical field—such as a dentist—might work for you. Of course, there are many professional options. I have just chosen these as examples.

Answer the Second of the Two Key Questions

You've priced your vision, so you now have the answer to the first question you must answer as you develop your life plan. How much money do you want to make? The second important determination is what you DON'T want to do.

One method of determining what you don't want to do is to estimate the likelihood of yielding the results you desire. One of the biggest struggles organizations face is finding a leadership team that will accomplish their objectives. This occurs when the vision from the top does not filter down to lower level managers. And if you currently are at the $40,000 mark, that manager may be your direct superior.

If you are working for a manager whose objectives are not aligned with the organization's objectives, it is unlikely that you will achieve positive attention from key decision makers. This may be due to that supervisor's own conflicts (which may have nothing or everything to do with you), or their unwillingness to give you the visibility needed to become noticed. If you find yourself in a situation similar to this one, you must decide if you want to be noticed or not. If you want an opportunity to be promoted, changing environments must be an option. This can mean changing organizations inside the current environment or changing employers.

Address Cultural Challenges

You may be employed by a typical corporation and have to push your company to a cultural change—one that would revise how the organization conducts its appraisals. Most organizations adhere to the standard of a performance appraisal. It is designed to manage an industrial workforce, to look back at the end of the year and correct deficiencies in performance. The problem with this form of assessment is that it was designed for industrial work, but we're no longer an industrial based economy.

Most of the high-paying jobs are knowledge based. But this assembly line performance mantra focuses on how often you arrived late to work, how often you took more than a fifteen minute break, and anything else your supervisor could come up with because he or she is, of course, rushed. You then get a score that will determine if you get a raise at the end of the year.

It is your objective to get your employer to abandon this form of performance appraisal, for it is designed NOT to get you a $60,000 increase. What you want is to be able to negotiate with your manager so you both can look at where you are at the beginning of the year and where you want to be at the end of the year. You want to get your employer to commit and formalize agreed-upon measurements. If you meet those measurements, you acquire what was agreed upon. Such an agreement could range from your moving to another position with the same pay but more upward mobility. Or, it could involve putting you in a fast-track training program.

If you are with the right company—one that doesn't fall over at the thought of increasing your pay $60,000 if you're worth it—then they will understand exactly what you're doing, and likely will admire you for it. So, another objective is to search out progressive-thinking organizations.

If you are in a position and shrouded by stumbling blocks, or even in a job that fails to embrace your values and stakeholders, you have come a long way in determining what you don't like. By figuring out what you don't like, you will be better able to determine what you DO like. As you go to work every day, keep close watch of two items: job openings that you feel you DO like within your current organization and opportunities in other corporations that better fit your personality and goals.

In real-world terms, this simply means the possibility of changing jobs or even careers. You will find that changing gears within yourself is a lot easier than changing your external environment, and considerably easier than trying to get a company to make your life priorities its number one concern. If your objectives are indeed important to you and your current career choices fail to match them, you have to be willing to adjust the job or career to fit your stated objectives—not only for your stakeholders but to maintain the integrity of your personal vision. It's okay to revise choices. It is not okay to stick with bad choices, refuse to correct them, and throw your own objectives out the window.

You Are Negotiating From Two Positions

Be mindful, however, of your true standing in any job. Whenever you are working for an organization, you're automatically negotiating from a position of weakness; any company can overcome the departure of a single individual, sometimes to their detriment. Even if you have the best interest of the organization at heart—and you should, always—they still may not have the willingness or ability to listen to you. Once you achieve positive attention from decision makers, they have the power to change your life in an instant. They can make discretionary promotions and give you a huge raise. You may be the one person correctly answering the million-dollar question, which is, "What value can you bring to this organization?"

But there are two sides to every story. If you have developed to the point where you bring value to any organization, then you also are working from a position of strength—they need you as much as you need them. It is important, therefore, to be keenly aware of your worth in your profession and in your organization so that you can command the higher income you seek. Never take this for granted. Always operate humbly and honestly. You can be replaced.

Dealing With Other Challenges—So What If You're Not 25!

There are numerous kinds of tough choices. For example, if you are middle-aged and in the middle of your work life, things are happening—marriages, children, tuition, and so on. You may have had a vision of being an executive in your organization, but your marriage soured and the negativity wormed its way into your work life.

I hold no position on marriage, divorce, or any personal challenges you may face. But let's say you're in a challenging marriage. You seldom fight with your spouse, but the fight is within because in spite of all your dreams, the marriage is not what you envisioned. To cope, you may find yourself involved in all types of destructive behavior and unfortunately, participating in every activity except the ones that would advance your life. A tough choice in this case would be to seek therapy or counseling before rushing off to meet the next objective.

What if you discover you're not the parent you always wanted to be, or that you have not upheld your responsibilities as you would have desired? You reflect and realize you have been coasting, and you realize this is unhealthy. One year turned into five, and five years turned into 10. You look back with dismay because nothing has changed over 10 years, yet you still have the burning in your heart to live out your vision.

Another hard choice is when you're having fun on your job, but a fun job is not in the plan. Here you are, two years into your plan and on track, and you absolutely love the people you work with. However, the company is going nowhere fast, the management team is unresponsive to your ideas, and you haven't had a raise since you started. Do you stay there and enjoy yourself or make a tough choice to leave and find another company that honors your plans?

The answer to these types of situations may lie within. It is my contention that God has a perfect plan for each of our lives and He gives us that vision in our most quiet times. It is up to us to honor that vision.

What About Big Challenges?

What about the person who has made some mistakes—encounters with the criminal justice system, a bad divorce, or even hitting rock bottom through drug addiction or alcoholism? It is still your choice to decide if you are going to go up from this point forward.

Now, the perfect plan—the one that your Higher Power has brought you into this world to achieve for your life—may not be totally accessible, but you can come very close. You have to decide if you are willing to put in the work necessary to have the best life possible from now on. There is no obstacle out there that hasn't been overcome already by someone else. Just look around: Venus or Serena Williams, who as children didn't have the privilege of playing tennis on a cushy court, practiced their way out of Compton playgrounds to become world champion tennis players. Bernard Hopkins spent time in prison and later became the undisputed middleweight boxing champion, with a record number of title defenses.

A Personal Example

You may run across situations where you are on track to meet your financial objectives, only to find that the track you're on doesn't mesh with your long-term goals. If you make money quickly, your immediate temptation may be to grab the money and run, shouting "See ya later, objectives. I'm rich!"

In such cases, it would be difficult for the two objectives to coexist. You have to be objective about your personal and long-term objectives. For example, my vision was to live a leisurely life on the coast of Florida by the time I was 50 years old. I created this vision when I was 25. I wanted to retire at 50, so every economic decision I made from that point on was based on that vision.

When starting my company, I had two choices. One was to run an organization and extract profits regularly. This meant I would need to operate with a minimum number of staff so I could maximize my own income from the company. The other approach would have been to take as little salary or income as possible. This would allow me to invest in the company to build value and equity, which would position it to be sold for the largest amount possible. The second option, however, would facilitate my long-term goal of early retirement.

I also had to face other tough choices. For instance, I developed my personal life plan at the age of 25. One of my objectives was to earn $100,000 by the age of 30. My salary was $40,000 annually at that time. However, I failed to reach my objective. Keeping my long-term goal in mind, I was forced to quit a job working for a company where I likely would have been very comfortable financially for the next 20 years. To make matters worse, once I quit that job, my base salary was reduced from $60,000 to $35,000. However, I had an opportunity to make commissions. My objectives kept me on track. If I had not shown respect for my own goals, I would have simply decided my objectives weren't worth the trouble. The cultural context from my childhood would have convinced me that keeping this job would be smart and comfortable.

Making decisions that are consistent with your objectives is an exercise in courage. I covered the foundation of faith in the chapter on cultural context—it's an inside job, starting with belief in yourself.

The Final Test—Appraise YourSELF

Most organizations employ some form of appraisal system to evaluate employees, but the most important appraisal is the one you give yourself. You can test the viability of your personal life plan by setting up periodic checkpoints to see how well the plan is working. This entails outlining your development over a 12-month period of time and using it to define what you hope to accomplish in one calendar year. Again, it basically makes an assessment of your personal position at the beginning of the year and measures your position against where you want to be within one year. It also serves as a means of filling in the gaps where needed. This is crucial because your time should not be idle during the year. Developing yourself prepares you not only for the next stage of growth, but for a wealth of opportunities that are bound to arise as others notice your development.

For example, if you are working in benefits now and want to be a VP of HR, you may be required to obtain a master's degree. In this case, you would give yourself three years to complete the master's. Concrete plans such as this help you ensure you are developing personally so that you can successfully take on the increased responsibility you desire.

Every employee should look at their life in the beginning of the calendar year and determine if they should make significant changes. Did your employer honor his or her promises? Should significant changes be made in your own development to achieve your objectives? If the employer honored his or her promises, is the job adversely affecting your health or family life? Do you feel frustrated and unhappy in this job? As you reflect on your decisions, the best you can hope for is to be able to hold up a mirror and make decisions that are best for you and your stakeholders in the long run. Developing a life plan takes lots of work and guts. As you scrutinize your vision, you may be tempted to end your analysis right there. Unless pressured by extreme circumstances, this is a task many of us would rather avoid. Those who complete their plan and follow through with their objectives, however, seldom fail.

Here is an example of the simple plan that I put in place when I was 25 years old and the decisions that I made to support what was important to me:

Objectives:

1. Get a job in computer sales.

2. Increase my income from $40,000 to $100,000 by the time I was 30.

3. Stakeholders—my future family. Give my future wife an opportunity to work optionally.

4. Finish my degree in computer science and marketing.

Decisions/Actions:

1. Get a job in computer sales. Express interest in sales at every level of management that would listen. They did not give me the job due to my lack of sales experience; however, they continued to give me training in sales to prepare me.

2. Increase my income from $40,000 to $100,000 by the

time I was 30. My company paid cash profit sharing, so my income jumped to $63,000 by the time I was 30. Because I did not reach my objective of $100,000, I took another sales job with a different company with a base salary of $35,000 and an opportunity to earn commissions. My income that year was $70,000, so I was closer to my objective. I changed jobs after that year and earned $114,000 when I was 31.

3. Stakeholders—my future family. Give my future wife an opportunity to work optionally. I married when I was 30.

4. Finish my degree in computer science and marketing. I enrolled in college and attended school at night and on weekends. I finished my bachelor's degree in computer science and marketing when I was 30. This also helped with my confidence during the interview process for a new job.

This plan is very simple, and I believe that its simplicity helped with its effectiveness. There were a few objectives that I set and could not deny success or failure. The lesson I learned through this process was that I had to be true to my objectives. The company I left when I was 30 was very prestigious. That feeling of belonging to something important made it difficult to leave. However, after exhausting all of my options with the company and giving them probably more years than I should have, I decided that the prestige they offered was not worth giving up my objectives. My move into sales at a smaller, lesser-known company enabled me to work in an area where I had a special gift. This made life much easier for me, and I was able to spend more time at home while gaining valuable experience in sales and management. This experience enabled me to start my own company within five years.

I failed at the objective that I set to make $100,000 by the time I was 30. However, because I made difficult decisions, I achieved that objective and more one year later.

Never allow anyone to steal your dreams. You have to honor them, take them seriously, make decisions, and take actions to support them.

Exercises:

1. Specify your five-year target income.

2. Slice your income target into manageable objectives (years).

3. Find someone that has accomplished what you want to achieve and schedule an appointment to discuss his or her journey with them. If they will not help you, find someone else. This can help you to avoid many mistakes.

4. Do your personal plan that addresses the development you require to achieve your 5 year income objective.

5. Determine how your targets track with your employer's available jobs that you desire. If you are self-employed, then write your objectives for your company/self.

6. Address your one-year milestones to track your progress.

CHAPTER 7
WHEN IS YOUR PLAN SUCCESSFUL?

Most folks are about as happy as they make up their minds to be.

—Abraham Lincoln

What is "success"? And while we're at it, just what motivates us to succeed? Prestige? Power? Pomp and prosperity? More than likely, if you ask two million people, you'll get two million different answers. Success is personal, but there may be some agreement that as a means unto itself, it does not automatically guarantee happiness.

So why take the time and energy to develop and carry out a life plan if it doesn't lead to some form of satisfaction? This is the tricky part, and it's even more personal—executing a life plan is a process of discovering what is truly important in *your* life. It is the process of finding out what really makes us tick that often leads us to contentment.

For many of us, the process of self-discovery is totally foreign, particularly if we are prone to follow in our parents' footsteps without much thought. Even then, we are likely to discover nuances about ourselves that we've never even considered, such as listening to Bach when we grew up with B.B. King or vice versa.

Implementing your life plan puts you in the general vicinity of what matters to you. This is the most productive posture to be in when making important decisions. Instead of using excess energy every day to decide the best course of action, you are now in no-brainer mode. You pretty much know where you stand on any given issue. Whether you choose to make a decision or flounder, the process of *Living Your Life Backward* gives you significant and sound options.

I define success as achieving objectives and values that are most important to you. Success is multidimensional because you will make a range of decisions, such as how much money is enough for you and your family, and the actual cost to you and your family for that desired level of success.

This chapter looks at the challenges and victories you will face as you evolve through your life plan.

It's Only Natural

One of the major challenges you will face is balancing your own idea of success with your natural tendencies associated with success. For example, human nature will tempt you to explore each level of success for the spoils of victory they hold. To illustrate, let's say you made $50,000 a year ago and you're now at the point of making $100,000. Now that you have "succeeded" in achieving your monetary goal, why shouldn't you have access to the many perks that $100,000 can buy? Or, human nature may suggest to you that you are more attractive to others now that you earn $100,000. Human nature says that you deserve to live in a different neighborhood and surround yourself with various luxuries, now that you earn $100,000.

If you are prone to grandiosity, you may question your pre-established mantra of success, which includes none of the above. At such junctures, you may step back only to discover that you actually enjoy that Toyota, even if you can now afford a glitzy Mercedes, and that you are still successful! You may realize that you are attractive whether you make $100,000 or $1 million, just because your wife, husband or significant other thinks so. You discover that you love the city life even if the house in the suburbs would impress your family and friends or vice versa. You're no longer in the right vicinity—you're right on target! Why? Because you've discovered what brings you contentment, and therefore you're a success.

The "Now What?" Syndrome

The moment will come when you achieve a milestone that shouts, "I've made it! Now what?" Some of you may experience the somber sensation that your journey is downhill from that point of success. For example, one of my objectives was to own my own company and do business with the U.S. government. By the end of my first year, I received a great number of contracts. For me, this was a significant milestone because I was then in the arena to compete for more lucrative government contracts. My first inclination was to shout this news over the mountaintop, and in my own way, that's exactly what I did. The person on the other end of that mountain happened to be a bank teller, to whom I duly announced, "I just found out today that

I could become financially independent." Her polite expression of "Oh-kay!" had little impact on my feeling that I'd "made it over the hump."

For some, this pivotal point may involve finally closing a significant venture capital deal, securing financing for a home from the bank, or paying off the mortgage on a home. The significance of the milestone depends solely on the objectives and goals laid out in your life plan.

The important thing to note about the unexpected challenges surrounding the achievement of some of your objectives is that they often accompany success and are not reserved for people who earn in excess of $1 million per year. Keep in mind also that such challenges will potentially revisit you at each significant, incremental level of success.

When such issues arise, it is my advice that you stay on course with your objectives or life plan and seek comfort in those who are closest to you and have demonstrated love over the course of your life.

You Got More Than You Bargained For

At this juncture, you need to realize that your objectives have gone from abstract to concrete. You have made a huge leap—from the mustard seed of a vision, which required faith, to operating on it. Once you begin to realize these milestones, your challenge is not so much in believing in the vision and the objectives, but living on proof obtained by historical achievements.

How Do You Know When to Change Your Life Plan?

Earlier, I described the notion that working on a plan is a way of discovering one's true desires in life. As you accomplish your goals, you begin to enter uncharted territory. Once you begin to achieve your objectives, you may tip the scales toward grandiosity. You may also be disappointed to find that many others do not exactly celebrate your success. However, it is important to return your focus to your priorities and what matters most.

One of the most magical discoveries about a life plan is when you find that your priorities are balanced with your family's values. When you are faced with situations that are not aligned with your vision, you intuitively know when to change course. A case in point is when you have established that the true cost of an increased income for your children's education is not a good total value proposition for your family. For example, your objective 10 years ago was to send Johnny to Harvard. You knew you'd need to make $250,000 annually to pay for his college education and maintain a certain lifestyle, but you later discovered that earning this $250,000 meant you had to miss every one of Johnny's soccer games.

At that point, you discovered that success was not Johnny's attendance at Harvard, but your attendance at Johnny's games. Your objective then changed—you instead put Johnny in an environment where he could earn his way to Harvard, or you might have discovered that there were other educational options. This impacted your life plan because your objective changed from having a net worth of $5 million at a cost of 14 hours a day to working in an executive position at a cost of nine hours a day, plus a relationship with your son. Meanwhile, you were aligning your priorities with your employer's objectives, which positioned you for upward mobility and perhaps even more flexibility in your scheduling.

The important piece here is that you have ensured that your objectives remained in line with your personal principles, even if this involved change. On the other hand, you were also prepared to change companies if your current one failed to match your new objectives.

By contrast, you may find that your area of talent is yielding a lucrative business. Yours may be of the philanthropic nature, and your family value is to help those in need. Here, you may discover that your tastes are such that you can enjoy making $250,000 annually and spending $50,000 a year on your lifestyle and charitable ventures. You are in a position to cut down on the time you devote to work simply because you have found a balance between earning plenty of money on the job, sharing, and just enjoying business.

You Are the Only Judge

A big part of living out your life plan is self-discovery and finding a balance that makes sense for you and your family. You are thriving in the midst of significant choices, but only after discovering the formula that works for your life.

Whether you achieve a bank account of $10,000, $100,000, $1 million, or $1 billion, the temptation to embrace society's values and ideas will be ever present.

You may be encouraged to earn dollars to keep up with the Joneses at the expense of your family. This is often a likely scenario because putting family ahead of success goes counter to many of society's values. It is not an understatement to note that society embraces a culture in which people make economic objectives without considering any other factors, as though achieving economic success will create a utopian environment. These are issues you will have to explore personally in your journey of self-discovery, even if you have descended from a family that possesses significant resources.

The subtleness of these challenges should not be underestimated, nor should you ignore the revelations that spring from them. I discovered the importance of insightful reflection soon after purchasing my "dream" home. While finalizing my divorce, I signed off on my property settlement, which allowed me to purchase a home that would be unencumbered by my past. This home met all of the criteria for my own definition of success. I finally had a place I could call home.

After settlement, and upon realizing the magnitude of this transaction, I stood in my foyer, viewing my beautiful home. I asked myself, *What have I just done?* The size of the home overwhelmed me simply because no one in my family had owned a home larger than 1,500 square feet. There I stood, with absolutely no concept as to what anyone would even do with all this space.

It did not take long to figure out that a media room, living room, dining room, a gym, a guest room, my daughter's bedroom, and an office absorbed all of the living space. I then realized that we would use as much space as was available in that house. I later understood that the vast amount of space eventually led to a point of diminishing returns—where space became wasteful.

The successful part for me was that my painful divorce was truly a low point in my life and I wanted so much to continue to provide a normal environment for my three-year-old daughter. This house provided a yard for her to play in and a place we could both build into our home. After my divorce, I was very bitter. However, because I had a life plan and was somewhat on autopilot in my career, I could deal with every distraction and get right back on track. It provided a source of relief sometimes, because I could be focused on good priorities in the midst of tremendous hurt. All in all, though, things did turn out pretty well.

Your Best Success—You

When you focus your attention and efforts on your own life plan, your self-awareness becomes acute as you investigate deep areas of yourself that have never been considered. Your desires likely will evolve or change—at one point you may wish to aspire to wealth, at another a more fulfilling career. It is my experience, however, that everything, with the exception of my relationships with God and my loved ones—has fallen short of my expectations. This in no way means my accomplishments have no merit or value. But it has put each of them into reality, and therefore into orderly perspective. More importantly, this self-discovery has shown me without a doubt what truly matters in my life. This awareness cuts me the biggest break of all—realization that as I evolve, I will always remain a work in progress.

CHAPTER 8
THE STORIES

This chapter features the stories of people I encountered through out my life. Each journey is very different from the other. Each person has dealt with a different set of circumstances. Each of them came up with a plan and executed it to improve their quality of life. They have provided some inspiration for me and I hope their stories are able to provide the same for you. In addition to their stories, I have included a couple of pages on my life's journey.

STORIES

The Gerry Kolosvary Story

Breaking away from the steel mills, he chose education and built a lucrative career in the computer field.

Cultural Context

I grew up in McKeesport, a small, blue-collar town just outside of Pittsburgh, Pennsylvania. Like most people in the area, my dad made his living off of the steel mills, working as a brakeman to support a wife and four kids. Mom brought in a minimal salary as a housekeeper at a local hospital.

We weren't *Happy Days*, but we ran a close second. Dad believed in paying his bills on time and putting something aside each payday. The mills paved the way for a pretty decent living—good benefits and all. You worked, saved for a rainy day, and then retired with a good pension, some small form of Social Security, and your life savings.

My father was very thrifty with money, if not extremely cautious. A product of the Great Depression, he understood the value of a dollar from not having one for a long period of time. I remember how once, I really wanted this Barracuda jacket with a price tag of $22.50. My father absolutely refused to pay that kind of money for that type of jacket in the mid-60s, so I had to get an imitation jacket. And using Visa to buy it was out of the question—the only items my father purchased on credit were second-hand family cars, and believe me, he paid those off as quickly as possible. It's funny his being that way may be why I turned out the opposite; strange things happen like that.

If my father wanted something expensive, he saved for it and bought it. It wasn't unusual for families to buy boats or vacation homes at nearby Deep Creek Lake. Such purchases, however, were seldom viewed as investments, but as the reward for working hard most of your life. There was no philosophy of becoming independently wealthy or saving enough cash so that money was not a concern, and the term "stock market" was absolutely foreign. Simply put, a strong work ethic was the key to survival and a good life. If you wanted anything, you had to earn it.

As far as most folks were concerned, the only option for earning this good life was a job at the mills. Top salaries ranged anywhere between $40,000 and $50,000—huge money back in the 60s and 70s. When we graduated from high school, the path was already set—get one of those high-paying jobs at the mills. And that's what most of us did, including my brothers and sister. Very few kids left the area and went to college.

I wanted to go to college, but there seemed to be a myriad of reasons not to. Topping the list was the fact that I was 18 years old and stone broke. Throw in my parent's flat-out rejection of the idea, and my chances were looking pretty nil. My family simply couldn't afford it, and why attend college when the mills provided a good living? Their take on college was exacerbated by the fact that most of the college graduates we knew came back as teachers making half the salary of people who worked at the steel mill. The funny thing about all this is that while in high school, my so-so grades were never an issue. The only time I faced trouble was if I misbehaved, and then we'd have a problem.

My uncle was the first person I knew to dispel the myth about the mills. As a kid, we'd visit him at his home in a beautiful place called Mentor on the Lake. He used to fly a P-51 Mustang during World War II, and when he'd come down to visit us, he'd always have lots of interesting stories to tell about serving as a fighter pilot. At the time, he was using his flying experience as an officer of a business. His company was doing some interesting things such as overhead mapping, using crude photography to take pictures.

This uncle was both my idol and mentor growing up. He had graduated with a degree in accounting from Duquesne University in Pittsburgh and would tell me that college was the ticket to a better life. He seemed to get a kick out of living and had the means to get just about anything he wanted. I wasn't crazy about the accounting idea, but I saw a huge difference in what he had and what others had. And I knew he had achieved his status by going to college.

My Life Plan

Going to college became the most important goal in my life, but I still lacked the means and the family backing to go. One way to get around this and attend college free was through the Armed Services.

I joined the Army for four years and earned my college degree in three and a half, using the GI bill. Wherever I was stationed, I went to school, starting with the University of Maryland in Munich, Germany.

Still basically broke and having to foot some of the bill, I attended the least expensive institution and graduated from George Mason University, a state school, with a degree in political science.

I majored in political science because I had big plans on becoming an attorney. The only problem was, I had no money for law school, and I needed a job. In my senior year, one of the recruiters that came to the campus was a company called Burroughs Corporation, a business process oriented company that sold business forms. This was a big industry because before the era of copiers and fax machines, people used forms to conduct all commerce.

Deciding that I could sell paper and business forms as a way to save for law school, I signed up for an interview on campus with a guy named Mr. Thompson. However, he canceled the interview because only a few people on campus had signed up. I was married by this time and had a double motive—to save money for law school and prove to my wife that I could work. So, I followed up with Burroughs, calling and asking to speak with Mr. Thompson. We set up the appointment and about 40 minutes into the interview, he asked a very peculiar question: "What makes you think you could sell computer systems?" Computers? Sell? I told him I couldn't. Turns out there were two Mr. Thompsons, and I had gotten the wrong one. I assumed I was interviewing with the Glenn Thompson, from the business forms department. Harry Thompson, however, headed the computer group, and he thought I'd do pretty well selling computers. I learned then that plans don't always go according to the way we set them.

A Change in Plans

This turned out to be a lucrative decision. The computer field was jumping and business forms were headed toward a bust. There was so much money in this field that I put the law school idea on temporary hold, still making plans to become an attorney one day.

While at Burroughs Corporation, making lots and lots of money, I changed my goal. My objective became, and still is to this day, to maintain a high level of income and find ways of creating additional stock through purchases, grants, or options. I measured each career move with this in mind and only worked for companies that paid high salaries and had lots of equity. Once I established relationships in this field and achieved a financial goal, I would begin to take a look at possible next moves down the line and alter my plans to take advantage of profitable opportunities.

My Key Strategy—Development and Knowledge

This was in the late 70s and early 80s—a period of rapid growth in the data processing industry. It was at this time that I changed my ambition, which was to continue to be as successful as I could be in the computer business. I began working at Tektronix, selling what turned out to be the crude but fundamental predecessor to the personal computer. I then moved out of selling and into management, progressing to the director level. I left Tektronix and joined a small start-up company called Silicon Graphics Inc., where I again made lots of money and equity.

I kicked off what I thought was my strategy when I was 21 years old and totally without experience in the world. My initial idea was to go to law school and become a lawyer. I thought that working for a DA's office or becoming a public defender would be a great idea. It was serendipitous for me to go to the wrong interview at Burroughs Corporation because neither of those careers pays much money, and the intrinsic rewards are very sporadic as well.

I discovered, however, that preparation, knowledge, and experience will determine success. When I landed the job at Burroughs Corporation, it was selling computers that did accounting. I took two basic accounting courses in college but did not have the detailed knowledge to set up a general ledger, accounts payable, accounts receivable, inventory, and payroll. So, you bet I had to learn fast. I bought several books and took additional courses at Northern Virginia Community College. Within six months, I could talk fluently about accounting software and consult with the customers about how to implement Burroughs Computers in their applications.

I continued to learn, taking college level courses in accounting, an introduction to computers, and public speaking. I then took sales training from Lee Dubois, plus read every sales book I could get my hands on, including Dale Carnegie, Zeig Zeigler, and others. I was also very interested in books about success, and I read many biographies of famous businesspeople of the time. I even bought a book called *Dress for Success*, and I followed it to a tee.

It took about one year really to get the hang of things and several years to develop my own style.

Eventually, I developed the key elements that would make me very good at what I did. These included knowing the strengths and weaknesses of the product as well as the competition, being able to describe complex engineering issues in a common sense fashion, being excited about the product, creating a contagious response from the customer, and selling against the competition without ever mentioning them by name or talking bad about them. I've learned that success or failure in this business is largely self-determined, but only the successful people are willing to admit that!

I continued working at various firms, building networks at each and continuing to leverage for higher salaries and equity. From SGI I went to FORE Systems, which was later acquired by Marconi. Marconi provided me with tremendous income and equity. I later became president of Marconi Communications Federal.

This strategy has worked for me, and I continue to build on it to this day. I am in the process of starting my own company and am partnering with another gentleman to start a second company. Both have the potential for tremendous income and equity. My plan is to make enough money someday to say, "I'm done."

Values Still Intact

I have been married for 33 years, and this was by far the wisest decision I have made in my life. Throughout the years, my wife has been my partner and involved in every decision along the way. We have two kids. Our daughter, 25, is a nurse and is having lots of fun. Our son is 21 and a sophomore in college. He's working on a business degree and we're hoping he'll have his own story to write someday.

There are many things that young people can do to prepare themselves. The first is to acknowledge an issue or shortcoming, the second is to do something about it. Knowledge and experience come with time, as you learn from your mistakes and successes. Success comes not from working "hard," but from working "smart." Know what it is that you need to do, and get it done. Don't become a victim of circumstances. There are many excuses for failure.

One of the most important lessons I've learned is that at the end of day, I might just fall on my face. But even if I'm a miserable failure, I can always go back and do something else. We always have to ask, "What's the worst thing that could happen?" With that, you pick yourself up, dust yourself off, and keep moving.

The Karen Lewis Story

This self-employed New York native leveraged her corporate knowledge into a lucrative property investment career.

Cultural Context

I was born and raised in Huntington Station, Long Island, and lived with my Mom, Dad, and brother for most of my life. We had a fulfilling childhood—my parents provided us everything we needed and some of the things we wanted. To me, we were doing just fine.

One thing I noticed was that my father worked—a lot. What I didn't realize was that my family was actually struggling, and my dad worked long hours to support us. He sheltered us from hardships that I didn't even know existed until I became an adult. I never knew how often he had held back on paying the electric bill so we could have school clothes, or gave up some other luxury to provide necessities.

One of the things I inherited from my father is a committed work ethic. I've always believed that if you work hard, you will do well. I had this concept when I entered college and carry it with me to this day.

Moving Forward—Fast

By the time I was about to graduate from college—two classes short of obtaining a bachelor's degree—I was full swing into corporate America as a senior manager for Coca Cola Enterprises. I was married to this job, never taking sick leave, never taking vacations, just immersing myself into getting ahead. I was what you'd call a rising star—being promoted every year over a four-year period—and seriously on the fast track.

Upon arriving at senior management, I had a few rude awakenings, and none of them were comfortable, to say the least. It was there that I saw how politically the corporate game was played.

Re-evaluating My Strategy

In 2000, I had begun looking at the idea of owning property so I wouldn't have to work in corporate America. I had a great deal of training and work experience from starting at entry-level positions and progressing to senior management in four years. During this career, I knew that one of my strengths was connecting with people. I figured, if I was making the company so much money by connecting with others, why not make my own money doing the same thing?

Meanwhile, I continued taking college courses, which were paid for by my company. This was my way of playing the corporate game—as long as I continued taking courses and gaining knowledge, I would continue being promoted.

My first purchase was a two-family, multi-dwelling unit in Queens. Everyone I told about this screamed, "Don't buy!" But I had done my homework and it looked like a good deal to me. I paid $290,000 for the house in 2001. It is now valued at $630,000.

I left corporate America. I now buy houses and rent them out. I do my financials and pay the mortgages on these houses from the rent I collect. I began buying more and more properties, taking equity from one home and using it to purchase another. Recently, I began managing properties out of state, so now I'm a property manager, too. When the houses peak in value, I try to sell them off. I currently own six multi-families, collect 20 rents a month and have a significant net worth.

It's Never Too Late to Learn

As I said earlier, my family struggled financially, and one thing of note is that my brother and I were never told how to manage money. What has made me successful in my current work is that I always figure out the numbers before making a purchase. I learned how to do such financials while in corporate America. I realized that many companies provide a lot of professional training, and I thought that if I didn't take those trainings and use them for myself, in all areas of my life, then they were useless for me.

There is always a way to learn from any situation. Get as much knowledge out of a company as possible, because they are paying for you to get it. However, at some point, you should always use this knowledge to build something of your own so that if anything is taken from you, you never feel defeated. The best thing that ever happened to me was divorcing myself from the corporate world.

Giving It Back

I lost my dad in October 2005. He had lived a healthy life the last six years, after having an aortic aneurism. He had been taking care of my mom after she had a blood clot and a stroke. Now I have a responsibility because although she is able to get around, her condition is still child-like. Being self-employed allows me to be there for my Mom. Being an entrepreneur has enabled me to set up an environment where I can have good home health care.

It was the experience I gained in corporate America that helps me manage and juggle this responsibility. Without this management experience, it would be difficult. Now, my priority is to balance my life and still continue living it fully. I wouldn't want it any other way, because my mom is very comfortable and has the best of care. It really isn't hard if you secure yourself financially. All that's left is figuring out the details.

The John Mendoza Story

This Cuban immigrant refused to let cultural context prevent him from reaching success in the real estate arena.

Cultural Context

I was born in Cuba and immigrated to Miami, Florida when I was six years old. My grandparents, who were the first in the family to come to Miami, cleaned and ironed at hotels. They would save their money and send it to my mom and dad in Cuba so we could move here.

When Dad, Mom, my two brothers, and I arrived in Miami, we were very poor. As new immigrants, it was a struggle to make ends meet. My parents were always working or studying to get ahead so we could have a better life. Dad would do construction jobs while my Mom worked as a teacher and went to school. Mom eventually earned her bachelor's degree in education, then a master's, and later a doctorate degree. To this day, she still teaches in the Dade County public schools.

I was raised Catholic, regularly attending church with my mom. We were taught right from wrong and to do the right thing. Family was most important. We had many family get-togethers during the holidays. If someone needed something, family was always there. Once, when my uncle and his wife came here from Cuba, they lived in a room for a couple of months and then moved in with us in a four-bedroom, two-bath home, until they got on their feet. This was a normal expectation and given freely.

I attended public elementary schools and then a Jesuit college preparatory high school. There was never a doubt in my mind that I would attend college. This point was driven home to my brothers and me by my mom, who was continuing her education, and by teachers and family. My personal cultural context—being Cuban in America—was dispelled at that Jesuit high school. They made it a point to let me know one thing: "You're American now—and there's no difference between you and your competition." We heard about SAT scores from ninth grade until we graduated. By that time, I felt prepared to compete economically.

Lessons Learned the Hard Way

It was in the area of economics that I saw the widest cultural gap. My parents taught us to work hard, live within our means, and try to make investments that would pay off. But the investments my dad made—and there were many—never panned out. Simply put, Dad was an honest man but a bad judge of character. This was because he made economic decisions based on his Cuban culture. Where he came from, a man's word was his bond, and the verbal agreement had the strength of a written contract. He had no problem paying $10 for a job that everyone else knew was worth only $5. In Cuba, if you cheated someone and the word got out, you were ostracized.

But in America, contracts rule, and if it isn't on paper, it just isn't so. One of the first business lessons I learned from this was that in America, all deals must be done contractually and even more important, you have to keep a close eye on your investments.

Even more unfortunate was that my dad never learned how to use credit. He didn't realize that you cannot succeed economically without it because credit allows you to make equity, which enables you to increase your net worth and thereby leverage money. I know many people who spent their entire lives never undersanding how money works. They never understood that part of growing economically is being able to show what you're worth.

Making the Right Decisions

At the age of 18, I became a father. I continued my education and became a teacher. Before doing so, I had planned to go to law school, but I found that I enjoyed working with children. I earned a bachelor's degree in education and decided to get a master's also—then head to Washington, DC, to get a doctorate degree. I wanted to be a lobbyist and change the American education system. I now know that it was my teaching career that prepared me for the work I do today as a real estate investor. A lot of patience is required to work effectively with children, and I often must practice patience when working with challenging buyers and difficult deals.

While pursuing my master's, the head of the education program at the University of Miami continually encouraged me, and I became heavily involved in various programs there. Then the program head and I clashed, and this pursuit became extremely personal and difficult. I realized from that experience, and from being a teacher, that it would be tough to make changes in the education system. My wife at that time wanted to have kids and suggested I get into a career that paid more money.

Before getting full swing into real estate, I tried other fields of work. I obtained my personal training license, continually searching for a career with a bit of excitement that would make me happy. I evaluated the different types of work I could do and felt that real estate fit my personality. I had already been reading about the Miami real estate market and decided to get into this line of business.

I got my real estate license, started listing houses and representing customers on the purchasing end, and eventually progressed into real estate investment. I now am working on getting to the next level. I recently bought 45 houses and plan to start condominium conversion or subdivision development. I haven't looked back.

Keeping the Balance

My strategy has always been that life is good—do what you like and like what you do. It's nice to have lots of money, but it's better to like what you do and be able to do what you like for a living. I'm a people person; real estate puts me in personal contact with people all the time.

Above all, it's still about relationships, whether business or family. My grandmother, the one who cleaned hotels and ironed sheets so my family could come here, seems to have made one of the best investments—in family. She now lives in a condo that I own. She has her own space and is constantly surrounded by her children and their kids. Like I said, it's *still* about relationships.

The Suzanne Cardoso Story

Suzanne had to learn the financial rules of survival at an early age, after the loss of her parents.

Cultural Context

I lived in the Mount Pleasant area of Washington, DC as a kid, and then I spent my teenage years in Bethesda, Maryland. I attended Bethesda Chevy Chase High School.

I am a product of what some would call a *true* rolling stone. My dad had 18 kids, and to this day, I've only met and known one of my siblings—a brother with whom I'm still close. My mom died when I was 11 years old, and after that I lived with this lady from the church. Then, my dad died when I was 17, and I ran away from home.

My dad had informed me about my many sisters and brothers just before he passed away. To think— I've got sisters and brothers out there I don't even know. I have done some digging, but because my father was Cuban, the details have been sketchy at most. What's strange is that to this date, I've never met anyone with my father's last name: Cardoso.

Choosing to Move On

I ran away because I lived like Cinderella at the church lady's house—in charge of cooking, cleaning, and helping with her son (who I am also very close with to this day). There I was, 11 years old, feeling like an indentured slave. When my dad passed away, his coworker came to the home to give me the news and said that I could stay with him. I lived with him until I was about 19 years old. But at 18, I decided to purchase a home using the money I inherited from my parents as a down payment. At the time, I was working as an insurance agent and Roberta, my boss, inspired me to purchase my own home. This was in 1994.

It was then that I learned an important lesson about choices: you can be around people who can help you or who can hurt you. Roberta was there for me, as well as another friend, Wendell, who was Roberta's landlord.

But having lost both my parents at an early age, I had to grow up quickly. The will to survive had to come from within. I believe I developed a knack for making this work because I had no other choice—I had no one to rely on, so I had to find a way to make it on my own.

My Life Plan

I made many mistakes along the way and learned some big lessons—such as saving money for a rainy day. My biggest blessing has been my daughter and my biggest gift to her is my ability to support and care for her without struggling, as many single mothers must do. My biggest benefit overall, however, has been learning the value of equity. Yes, it's good to save for a rainy day, but investing is the way to build wealth and security. I purchase properties and when the time is right, I sell them and get the equity. I have not found any other way to make as much money on an investment—even if the property is kept for only a year. This can be a time-consuming process, but I'd do it over and over again.

I am currently a loan officer, and I love what I do. This career enables me to help other people's dreams come true. To see their eyes light up as they realize their dream—it really does something positive for me. If a person is unable to purchase a home, we have a credit repair program and other ways to help. What I like most about my career is the flexibility—I can attend my daughter's events, school activities, and be an active part of her life.

Never Say Never

Right now I have two investment properties, and I live in my third home. It's a nice living for me and my nine-year-old. I have been investing for about one year and see a bright future, with myself in control.

I didn't have the advantage of parents teaching me about money or economics; it was strictly "grow or go." The message I'd like to pass on to you and to my daughter is not to have to depend on anyone. You can do anything you want if you set your mind to it—because only the strong survive.

My Story

Focusing on a faint vision of entrepreneurship using all means possible to escape a poor urban existence.

Cultural Context

I was born in Milwaukee, Wisconsin, the fourth of six children raised in a single-parent home. My mom, sisters, brothers, and I lived in a three-bedroom house on Brown Street. The neighborhood was not the worst, but it had its fair share of crime, blight, and other non-amenities that were a normal part of the inner city. I attended public school most of my life, with a few years of private middle and high school.

We weren't rich, and I didn't feel poor. There was no talk of economics or savings or stocks, because most people worked low or mediocre-paying jobs and lived paycheck to paycheck. I got a rude awakening of our true economic status one day when my mom informed me that we were on "welfare." I detested this status and the sense of economic dependence that accompanied it. Even though I had no clue HOW I would overcome it, I made up my mind at that moment that this was NOT how I would live my life. I got a paper route and have never stopped working.

Gradual Improvements

Our financial status improved when my mom married my stepfather, Andrew, which is likely how I was able to attend a private school from eighth to tenth grade.

My stepfather elevated our lives financially through his steady job as a factory worker. He was an honest man with a solid work ethic, and he had surpassed many others in our economical circles. After graduating from high school, I got a sales job at J.C. Penney's. The work was mostly cutthroat commission and after all the blood, sweat, and tears, my take home pay was about $300 per week. As far as my family was concerned, I had hit pay dirt. I was making GOOD MONEY! Throw in the illusion of wealth that a good suit can provide, and I really had it made!

My Life Plan

What woke me up was witnessing a salesman attempt to sell skates to my employer. The man walked away with $3,000—ten times my salary. I decided I was on the wrong side of the selling table, and that I didn't need to sell FOR Penney's, I needed to sell TO Penney's. That $3,000 commission check whetted my appetite, and I haven't been the same since.

My financial status remained the same, and one way out was through the military, which would fund my education. I joined the Air Force at 19. This introduced me to the computer field and seven years after my discharge from the Air Force, I earned a bachelor's degree in computer science and marketing.

Throughout the years, I gained as much knowledge as I could about the computer business. Although my jobs as a systems analyst and computer sales analyst paid well, my dream was to sell computer solutions. But this was a tough glass to break. At 25, I began setting short and long-term goals, which included learning how to run a business, becoming financially independent, and retiring by the time I was 50. I earned an MBA from Loyola College and opened Scientific & Engineering Solutions, Inc. in 1996. I built the company to about 200 employees and retired at the age of 44.

Today, I am a single parent, spending most of my time with my ten-year-old daughter in my primary home in Miami, Florida. I already have learned how to braid my daughter's hair, shop for and with her, and be a committed father and friend. Recently, I began taking acting lessons and producing a very contemporary gospel CD, things I always wanted to do.

I have the respect of my daughter, a few trusted friends, and a relationship with God. I know that God gave me a bigger vision than the one I was shown as a child, as well as the faith and strength to believe in that vision. The only difference between my story and many others is my unwavering faith that God gave me that vision, and therefore he would give me what I needed to achieve it. I never stopped acting upon the vision that God gave me. Everything I do, including this book, is a service to advance God's plan in my life. My relationship with God is the foundation for everything I do.

For further information, updates or
ordering additional copies, please visit:
www.livingyourlifebackward.com